Can You BE a Tea Party Member and STILL Call Yourself Christian?

(A Newly-Revealed Word of God for the Tea Party Generation)

by Bill Schmalfeldt

COPYRIGHT 2011
BILL SCHMALFELDT

ALL RIGHTS RESERVED. NO PART OF THIS BOOK MAY BE REPRODUCED IN ANY FORM, EXCEPT FOR THE INCLUSION OF BRIEF QUOTATIONS IN REVIEW, WITHOUT THE WRITTEN PERMISSION OF THE AUTHOR.

ISBN-13: 978-0615482750
(Deep Brain Productions)

ISBN-10: 0615482759

Published in the United States of America

(All accompanying illustrations are from the public domain, re-crafted by the author, unless otherwise indicated.)

DEDICATION

To the poor, unnamed slobs who labored with quill and ink over the original biblical texts only to see other guys get credit for their work, to the dozens of different committees over the centuries who translated then re-translated, then re-re-retranslated ad infinitum the sacred scripts into the current version of the unerring, word-for-word, never changing, not a jot, not an iota, even the parts that contradict each other texts, and the fellows who had to decide which book went in the Bible, which got tossed out, depending on who was King or Pope at the time. To everyone who lost his or her life because he or she interpreted these words the wrong way in the eyes of the guys with the guns or swords. To those of other religions who lived peacefully with their understanding of the universe until they were force-fed OUR religion at gunpoint, to those who call themselves Christian while still killing each other because YOUR brand of Christianity isn't the same as HIS brand of Christianity, the spirit of this book is dedicated. If there is anything to be learned here, LEARN IT before we all murder each other.

AND QUIT USING GOD'S NAME TO JUSTIFY YOUR HATRED OF OTHER PEOPLE!!!

OK? Thanks.

CONTENTS

1	How I Wanted to Be a Tea Partier…	1
2	The Problem	6
3	The Solution	14
4	Christian Charity	20
5	Caring for the Ill and Elderly	28
6	Miracles and Wonders	42
7	Gloom, Despair and Misery for the Non-Believer	48
8	Parables and Lessons	54
9	The Ten Commandments in a Tea Party Context	66
10	Whatsoever You Do to the Least of These	70
11	How About a Little Taste of the New Righteousness?	83
12	And All Mysteries Are Revealed	162
13	The Punch Line	201

ACKNOWLEDGMENTS

This book pretty much happened by accident. I had written a piece for my "Observations of a Brain Damaged Troll" column on the Technorati [1] website concerning the need to rewrite the Bible to fix the dichotomy between what Christian Fundamentalist Tea Party members SAY and what is actually WRITTEN in the Bible.

This column was seen by a literary agent in New York City who approached me with the idea of turning the column's central concept into a book. This lit the old fire in the brain, and before you know it I had some 250 pages of manuscript and several self-created illustrations. Well, somewhere along the line, either the agent lost interest in the project – maybe she's still considering it. I have no idea. But this was just too good of an idea to let it sit collecting dust on a computer hard drive.

So, this is the printing of last resort… as most of my other works have been. Manuscripts that I believe in, stories that I felt needed to be told. But the market being what it is for new writers, I can't say I blame a literary agent for not taking on a client who doesn't have a huge following or list of book sales to brag about.

That being said thanks for the idea Laurie. The copy of this book you're holding would not have been possible without your sparking the creative fire.
.

---

[1] 1 http://technorati.com/politics/feature/troll/

1 HOW I WANTED TO BE A TEA PARTIER...

I dearly wanted to be a member of the Tea Party. I truly did. I'm white, middle-aged, I hold some moderate-progressive views but I also think government spending has gotten out of hand. I'm a patriot, a veteran of nine years service in the United States Navy.

So when the Tea Party held a massive rally in Washington, DC, I went there. I tried to mingle with them. I tried to fit in. But I just couldn't do it.

My problem? I believe in God. I believed, at the time, his admonitions to us as revealed in his Holy Word, the Bible, that we should treat others as we wish to be treated, that we should care for the sick, that we should show charity to the poor, that whatever we do for the least of our brothers, it's as if we've done it for Christ Jesus himself.

These Tea Party members at the rallies I attended. They were carrying horrible signs. They were CURSING at African American congressmen, SPITTING on them, calling them NAMES! This report[2] tells the story...

---

[2] http://www.huffingtonpost.com/2010/03/20/tea-party-protests-nier-f_n_507116.html

A staffer for Rep. James Clyburn (D-S.C.) told reporters a protestor had spit on that Rep. Emanuel Cleaver (D-Mo.). Rep. John Lewis (D-Ga.), a hero of the civil rights movement, was called a 'ni--er.' And Rep. Barney Frank (D-Mass.) was called a "faggot," as protestors shouted at him with deliberately lisp-y screams. Frank, approached in the halls after the president's speech, shrugged off the incident.

But Clyburn was downright incredulous, saying he had not witnessed such treatment since he was leading civil rights protests in South Carolina in the 1960s.

"It was absolutely shocking to me," Clyburn said, in response to a question from the Huffington Post. "Last Monday, this past Monday, I stayed home to meet on the campus of Claflin University where fifty years ago as of last Monday... I led the first demonstrations in South Carolina, the sit ins... And quite frankly I heard some things today I have not heard since that day. I heard people saying things that I have not heard since

March 15, 1960 when I was marching to try and get off the back of the bus.

I went home feeling that this just wasn't right. It wasn't right at all!

I had been present at some of the great moments of the past. I heard Dr. King give his great "I Have a Dream" speech in 1963. I was 8-years old. I was 13 when Dr. King and Bobby Kennedy were murdered just weeks apart in 1968.

I had been raised by hard-working Democrats who believed in you had to earn your own way in life, but that God insisted we help those who were having trouble.

And here I was, in the middle of this screaming crowd of my fellow middle-aged white people. They were calling President Obama a communist. Calling him a Marxist. Calling him a Muslim. All of which, of course, are lies. These people, who to a person BENEFIT from the LBJ's "Great Society" which sprang from JFK's "New Frontier" were now being used as tools by a right wing machine, I felt, that fooled them into believing that they were NOT acting against their own best interest.

I went home depressed and disillusioned.

How can you call yourself a Christian and knowingly "bear false witness?" How can you call yourself a Christian and tell a sick person to "take care of himself because you won't do it." How can you call yourself a Christian and mock a person for the color of his skin?

None of it made any sense…

That is, until later that night.

An angel appeared to me in a dream. Dressed in glowing golden robes, the angel handed me a large volume of typed, double-spaced manuscript text. Courier New font, 12 picas.

GOD'S HOLY ANGEL DELIVERS THE MANUSCRIPT UNTO ME

"It is not the tea partiers who are wrong," the angel said. "It's their Bible. It's been misinterpreted. What you now have in your hands is God's word as He MEANT for it to be read. Go therefore unto the nation and the world; make them aware of this new, correct translation of God's word into the English vernacular, easy for the dimmest of your Tea Party people to understand. They commit nowrong in God's eyes. Tell them to keep up the good work and vote Republican in November."

The angel disappeared, and when I awoke the manuscript was still clutched in my hands. I leafed through it and, by golly, the angel was RIGHT! The Tea Partiers weren't violating God's word by calling for government to get out of their health care. They weren't being hypocrites for accepting Medicare and Social Security while hating those who receive other forms of Government assistance. Their racial prejudices, their inexplicable hatred of things they didn't understand. It was all right there. In God's NEWLY REVEALED WORD!

So, as the angel told me, it's time to go forth into the nations and the world and spread his NEW word. Greed is OK. It's not lying if you do it for a good reason. Theft is perfectly fine as long as the person you are stealing from is a sucker or otherwise deserves it. See for yourself in these pages.

2 THE PROBLEM

The Tea Party, the new faction of the Republican Party that claims they wish to "take America back from the Socialist, Marxist, Heathens and Communists," and return our country to the control of "Godly Men and Women" who understand that American was "founded on Christian, Biblical principles" have a basic problem – with the Bible.

Let me rattle off a few names:

Newt Gingrich. Former Republican Speaker of the House. Led the impeachment fight against Bill Clinton for lying about his sexual relationship with an intern. At the time, was cheating on his second wife with the woman who became his third wife. Cheated on his first wife with his second wife, serving her with divorce papers while she was in the hospital recovering from cancer surgery. He is calling for a Christian revival[3].

Newt Gingrich "warned that America is headed toward becoming a godless society unless voters take a stand against President Obama and liberal-minded college professors and

---

[3] http://elections.americablog.com/2011/03/gingrich-vs-godless-society.html

likeminded media pushing his agenda," the San Antonio News-Express reports.

He also "called for a return to historic, Christian roots he said were critical to protecting the nation's freedoms."

Said Gingrich: "There's a desperation with which our elites are trying to create amnesia so that we literally have generations who have no idea what it means to be an American."

Another name: **Mark Foley.** Former GOP congressman. Crusader against gay rights. Had to leave Congress after it was revealed he was sending and receiving sexually explicit and suggestive texts from underage male House pages.

OK. **Larry Craig.** Former Idaho Senator. Fellow anti-gay crusader. Plead guilty to lewd conduct in a Minneapolis airport bathroom while attempting to solicit oral sex from an undercover police officer.

Sen. **David Vitter,** (R-LA). While still just a congressman, this "family values" lawmaker was wrapped up in the "D.C. Madame" Prostitution Scandal where word was he enjoyed wearing diapers. Co-sponsor of the "Defense of Marriage Act." With Sen. Craig.

Former Sen. **John Ensign** (R-NV). Finally resigned two years into a scandal over having an affair with a campaign volunteer who was married to one of his staff aides. Ensign's parents gave the staff aide a $96,000 "gift." Ensign resigned when the Senate Ethics Committee made it crystal clear that expulsion from the Senate was the other option. Called for Clinton's resignation in 1994 because of the Lewinsky affair. Once called marriage[4] "an extremely important institution in this country and protecting it is, in my mind, worth the extraordinary step of amending our constitution."

The list goes on and on. **Rudy Giuliani. Henry Hyde. Mark Sanford, Jim Gibbons, Ted Haggard, Don Sherwood, Rush Limbaugh,** all purveyors and spokesmen for the "family values" wing of the Republican Party. All men who have had severe, public, "moral lapses." That's the portion of the party now occupied by the so-called "Tea Party."

And what about the founding members of the various Tea Party groups? **Dale Robertson,** for instance. Founder of Tea Party.org.[5] His website presents him as an All-American boy, a veteran of the Marines who believes "

---

[4] http://www.politicususa.com/en/Ensign-hypocrite

[5] http://www.teaparty.org/

The Tea Party dream includes all who possess a strong belief in the foundational Judaic/Christian values embedded in our great founding documents.⁶ He goes on to quote himself, "It was the Constitution that is inherently conservative, not a party. I believe there must be a beacon to the masses who have lost their way, a light illuminating the path to the original intentions of our Founding Fathers. We must raise a choir of voices declaring; America must stand on the values that made us great. Only then the politically blind shall see and the deaf shall hear!" All good words, Dale. Are THESE the kind of "values" you're talking about?

While at a Tea Party event on February 27, 2009, a photo was taken of TeaParty.org founder and president Dale Robertson with a sign that said "Congress = Slaveowner, Taxpayer = Niggar". It has been reported that he was ejected from the event because of the offensive nature of the sign, and Houston Tea Party Society leaders ousted him from the society shortly after. It was reported that Robertson intended to sell the domain TeaParty.org; however, as of November 2010 he is named the "President & Founder" on the TeaParty.org "About" section.⁷

It is currently 6:53 am EDT, April 29, 2011. He's still listed as described above.

My wife and I had the distinct pleasure of meeting Mr. Robertson on Feb. 14, 2009. We had decided to take a weekend vacation to Washington, D.C., just about 30 miles south from where we live. We strolled along Pennsylvania Avenue and saw ol' Dale there standing, holding his sign. Then, he put the flag he was holding down on the street so he could readjust his underwear – or something. I walked over to

---

⁶ http://www.teaparty.org/about.php#what

⁷ http://en.wikipedia.org/wiki/Tea_Party_movement

him as my wife gave me one of those "here he goes again" roll of the eyes.

"Pick up your flag," I said to him.

Like many cowards when they hear a deep, resonating voice giving a command, Dale (I had no idea who he was at the time) bent over and picked up the flag. Then he stopped and said, "And what does the flag mean to you, sir?" I replied it was the symbol of our nation and that since he was wearing a hat with the word "Navy" on it, he should know better than to disrespect it by letting it lie on the dirty street.

"But what about the disrespect Congress and the President show our Constitution every day..." he started to say, but I cut him off. "Oh, shut up. The people held an election. Obama won. Deal with it."

By this time, a crowd was gathering and my wife was pulling me away by my coat sleeve.

"THE CONSTITUTION GIVES ME THE RIGHT TO STAND HERE AND SPEAK MY MIND..."

"The Constitution gives you the right to kiss my ass," I said as my wife dragged me south on sidewalk adjacent to the East Wing of the White House.

Before the angel delivered the NEWLY REVEALED Word of God, this sort of thing used to torment me considerably.

Does the problem lie in the hearts of these men? Racism is certainly NOT a "Christian Value." At least not in THIS day and age. When they call themselves "Christian," are they lying? Or are they just misled?

I believe that most Tea Party members, the ones you see carrying signs questioning President Obama's citizenship, saying they want government off their backs (as long as they keep getting their Medicare, Disability and Social Security Checks) and protesting "Obama Care" (Your Health, Your Problem) are good, decent, misguided people with backwards racial attitudes that fall short of outright racism, but you seldom see them inviting black people over for dinner, let alone to their rallies. I believe most of these folks, poor-to-middle-class, elderly and white, lack the self-awareness necessary to realize the hypocrisy of claiming to be Christians while taking such abhorrently anti-Christian political stances. I believe the majority of them have been duped by an industrial machine that has lured them into supporting their efforts by taking the dog dropping of industrial deregulation, wrapping it in gold foil, slapping a picture of Ronald Reagan and a flag on it, and renaming it a "Patriot Bar."

The industrial interests behind the Tea Party could care less about these people and their eternal souls. But the average Tea Party member, no doubt, believes him or herself to be a "good person."

They claim America is a Christian nation, using quotes from founding fathers who believed the direct opposite. They claim Muslim sharia law is a threat to their American way of life, and they fear that this "outsider" in the White House may, probably IS, a Muslim Manchurian Candidate just waiting for the right opportunity to drag America into some worldwide caliphate.

These God-fearing, Christian Americans have one basic problem. They are at odds with what most folks perceive as the Holy Scripture.

The GOP Sex Scandals, for instance. Foretold!

24 Therefore God gave them over in the sinful desires of their hearts to sexual impurity for the degrading of their bodies with one another.

25 They exchanged the truth about God for a lie, and worshiped and served created things rather than the Creator—who is forever praised. Amen.

26 Because of this, God gave them over to shameful lusts. Even their women exchanged natural sexual relations for unnatural ones.

27 In the same way the men also abandoned natural relations with women and were inflamed with lust for one another. Men committed shameful acts with other men, and received in themselves the due penalty for their error.

28 Furthermore, just as they did not think it worthwhile to retain the knowledge of God, so God gave them over to a depraved mind, so that they do what ought not to be done.

> *29 They have become filled with every kind of wickedness, evil, greed and depravity. They are full of envy, murder, strife, deceit and malice. They are gossips,*
> *30 slanderers, God-haters, insolent, arrogant and boastful; they invent ways of doing evil; they disobey their parents;*
> *31 they have no understanding, no fidelity, no love, no mercy.*
> *32 Although they know God's righteous decree that those who do such things deserve death, they not only continue to do these very things but also approve of those who practice them.*

ROMANS 1:24-32

So, how in the world can one claim to be to be a God-fearing American patriot while supporting candidates for office that speak to a philosophy that is, on it's face, against practically everything these people BELIEVE Jesus preached about two eons ago.

All that stuff that told us about "loving your neighbor" and "forgiving their trespasses." How about "whatsoever you do to the least of these, my brothers, that you have done unto me." How does the average good, white, middle-class Christian American ALLOW him or herself to preach such hatred against foreigners and homosexuals when the Bible – as they know it -- specifically COMMANDS them to treat strangers with kindness, and says as much if not more against eating pork and wearing clothing made from mixed fabric as it does about homosexuality. They claim that Jesus brought a NEW testament to replace the Old Testament. So where does Jesus condemn homosexuality and immigration?

So, if your problem is that you want to call yourself a God-fearing, Bible-believing patriot that wants to return America to its Biblical roots (that never exactly existed), which is easier to do? Changing your heart? Or changing the Bible?

But I tell you, it is not NECESSARY to change either your heart OR God's word. The NEWLY REVEALED word of God shows that your hearts are already IN the right place.

Of course, it's a lot to expect that these simple, unsophisticated people who attend most of your Tea Party rallies are self-aware enough to UNDERSTAND that what they've been prattling on about is diametrically opposed to what they were taught in Sunday school.

That is why it is VITAL that the NEWLY REVEALED word of God soon REPLACES the standard texts in our churches.

3 THE SOLUTION

On that evening not long ago, before the angel appeared to me in the dream, in the usual half-hour I spend pondering the mysteries of the universe, I asked myself this question.
"What are Republicans good at?"
The answer came swiftly.
"Pretending they speak with the authority of God, and rewriting history to reflect their political agenda."
Oh my, yes! Is that ever true! Conservative "Christians" use the bible like a truncheon, to whack non-believers on the head with cherry-picked scriptures that support their point of view, while ignoring the ones they don't really cotton to. For instance, they LOVE to tell the gays they are hell bound by quoting Leviticus 20:13 — *"If a man also lie with mankind, as he lieth with a woman, both of them have committed an abomination: they shall surely be put to death; their blood [shall be] upon them."* What other gems of good behavior can we find in the King James Version (KJV) of Leviticus?

And if a man shall lie with a woman having her sickness, and shall uncover her nakedness; he hath discovered her fountain, and she hath uncovered the fountain of her blood: and both of them shall be cut off from among their people. (No making "uh-uh" during the "monthlies!")

Leviticus 20:18

And the man that committeth adultery with another man's wife, even he that committeth adultery with his neighbor's wife, the adulterer and the adulteress shall surely be put to death. (Wow! Only three verses away from the homo one! I'm lookin' at YOU, Newt and Trump!)
Leviticus 20:10

And the swine, though he divide the hoof, and be cloven-footed, yet he cheweth not the cud; he is unclean to you. Of their flesh shall ye not eat, and their carcase shall ye not touch; they are unclean to you. These shall ye eat of all that are in the waters: whatsoever hath fins and scales in the waters, in the seas, and in the rivers, them shall ye eat. And all that have not fins and scales in the seas, and in the rivers, of all that move in the waters, and of any living thing which is in the waters, they shall be an abomination unto you: They shall be even an abomination unto you; ye shall not eat of their flesh, but ye shall have their carcases in abomination. Whatsoever hath no fins nor scales in the waters, that shall be an abomination unto you. (So, that pork sausage and shrimp on the barbie? Verboten! That nice pork roast in the crock pot will SEND YOU TO HELL!!! It's in the BIBLE!!!)

Leviticus 11:7-12

But then, to justify their homo hate and pork love, Christians will say that Jesus brought a New Testament that CHANGED the law and made the OLD Testament obsolete... except for the parts they like! They say the NEW Testament ALSO forbids homo stuff.

OK, where does Jesus say a THING about it in the New Testament?

Come on, people... I need a chapter and verse here. WHERE does JESUS CHRIST have ANYTHING TO SAY, POSITIVE OR NEGATIVE about homosexuality?

What... nothing?

Oh, wait. Here's something.

And likewise also the men, leaving the natural use of the woman, burned in their lust one toward another; men with men working that which is unseemly, and receiving in themselves that recompence of their error which was meet."
Romans 1:26-27 (KJV)

But waitaminnit... *Book of Romans?* PAUL's letter to the Romans? *PAUL,* the former persecutor of Christians and scoundrel known as Saul of Tarsus until he had this sudden transformation and became a Christian? The one who never actually laid EYES on Jesus or heard a word He SPOKE? HE said that? Not GOD?

In fact, EVERY anti-homo utterance in the NEW Testament, the one that supplants the OLD testament, was written NOT by Jesus, NOT by GOD, but by this "Paulie Come Lately" who never met, never spoke to, never shared a cup of coffee with Jesus, and HIS writings are treated the same as if it were God Himself dipping His Almighty pen into the Eternal Ink of Enlightenment.

So, let's revisit my original hypothesis in this foreword.

What are Republicans good at?

Well, rewriting history is a given. Look at how they've fooled their followers into thinking the current economic crisis is OBAMA's fault. Yet, Obama created more jobs in 2010 than Bush created in his entire term.

These industrialists and their media tools have cleverly fooled the Tea Party into thinking this whole mess is OBAMA's fault. So we know they're great at rewriting history.

But when faced with the contradictions in their holy book, and the fact that outside of the Old Testament, God/Jesus has NOTHING to say, good or bad, about homosexuality, and BOTH parts of the bible speak to helping the poor, forsaking one's own wealth to help the less fortunate, caring for the sick… all totally ANTI-Tea Party positions where the poor can help themselves and quit leeching off the taxpayer… how do they resolve the conflict between calling themselves "good, Godly Christians representing a Christian Nation where we should return to the Christian Values that made us a GREAT Christian Nation" and their serial violation of the very things

God/Jesus COMMAND of them in the Old AND New Testaments?

As I drifted off to sleep, I saw no way to avoid this dichotomy. I resolved that one cannot be a Christian and preach hatred against his fellow human. One cannot be a Christian and deny his brother or sister decent health care, security in old age, or the basic necessities of life.

No doubt there will be some who read this who scoff at the idea that an Angel of God gave me a NEWLY REVEALED sacred text to replace the King James Version of Holy Scripture.

However, some WILL believe in the miraculous appearance of a new scripture that contradicts most of what they were taught in their early religious education. That's why we have Mormons.

But even for those who will be skeptical, I tell you… there is precedent. You think the King James Version fell out of the sky? No, my gentle reader. It was a collaborative effort in the 17th Century to correct the "past mistakes[8]" in previous translations of sacred scripture from the original Greek and Latin texts.

And what about the other ancient texts that didn't make the final cut? I mean, the so-called "Apocrypha[9]" – books written by the early Christians that were deemed unworthy to be included in the "final" revisions of the Bible. And even now, not every denomination agrees[10] on which books are "canonical," meaning they are accepted into the Bible, and "apocryphal", which are not.

This volume is not intended to be a scholarly biblical treatise or a discussion of what belongs in the Bible and what

---

[8] http://www.bible-researcher.com/kjvhist.html

[9] http://www.earlychristianwritings.com/apocrypha.html

[10] http://en.wikipedia.org/wiki/New_Testament_apocrypha

doesn't. I'm merely trying to pass on a version, given to me by an Angel of God, that members of the modern-day Tea Party can use, claim as their own, follow to the letter, and not be hypocritical. Call it a public service.

This first book will not contain the completely NEWLY REVEALED Word of God. Just bits and pieces to get the ball rolling. Just enough to give our "Your Health, Your Problem," and be able to point to chapter and verse where your Bible says the sick should take care of their own damn selves! See the value in this?

We'll call it "The Holy Bible — the Tea Party Version", or "TPV" to keep it short and abbreviated.

What will this new, contemporary, Tea Party scripture look like?

Here's a preliminary glance.

4 CHRISTIAN CHARITY

Tea Partiers are all ABOUT charity to the poor, unless — of course — they're being asked to pay for it. You can find a few who drop a buck into the Salvation Army bucket at Christmas time, or give their offerings to their church, which gives some to the poor if you're lucky; mostly it's used by the pastor for his TV time, his hair spray and to keep his mistress farting through silk.

Tea Partiers HATE it when their TAX dollars are used for charity, for welfare, for food and milk for babies, for health care. That's SOCIALISM, they screech. That's COMMUNISM. If we want to donate to something, that should be OUR choice, not the Government's!

The Tea Partiers PREACH a good game. But do they follow the biblical dictates of God, which command them to be charitable, to be aware of the poor around them, to help where they can?

According to the PREVIOUS Bible, NO! They do NOT! They clearly VIOLATE the texts that instruct them to give freely to the poor. But those verses in the KJV were mistranslated. This NEWLY REVEALED version will mesh much easier with the Tea Party member's base instincts.

For instance…

The afflicted and needy are seeking water, but there is none, and their tongue is parched with thirst. I, the LORD, will answer them Myself, as the God of Israel I will tell them to get a job and BUY some water. What are we? The free water people?

Isaiah 41:17. (TPV)

If there is a poor man among you, one of your brothers, in any of the towns of the land which the LORD your God is giving you, harden your heart, close your hand to your poor brother; you shall freely seek to profit from him, and generously lend him sufficient for his need at a subprime rate and then foreclose when he misses his first payment.

Deuteronomy 15:7. (TPV)

Do justice and righteousness, and deliver the ones who have been robbed from the power of the duly elected government. Also do not mistreat or do violence to the stranger, the orphan, or the widow unless absolutely necessary; and do not shed innocent blood in this place. Do it somewhere else, like in a nation that threatens thee not!

Jeremiah 22:3. (TPV)

"If thou desireth to sell your possessions, do so in a manner that will secure a tidy profit; make yourselves purses which do not wear out, an unfailing treasure on Earth, where no thief

comes near fearing your stash of weapons, nor oppressive tax rate applies."
Luke 12:33. (TPV)

But when you give a reception, do not invite the poor, the crippled, the lame, the blind, since they do not have the means to repay you and will verily disgust your guests.
Luke 14:12-14. (TPV)

"He has placed rulers on their thrones, and has exalted those who were wealthy, not from their hard work, but through inheritance. He has filled the haughty with good things; and sent away the poor empty-handed."
Luke 1:52. (TPV)

"But joy to you who are rich, for you are receiving your comfort in full, and deservedly so!"
Luke 6:24. (TPV)

"[The conservatives] do not plead the cause, the cause of the orphan, that they may prosper; and they do not defend the rights of the poor. Shall I not punish these people?" declares the LORD. "On such a nation as this, shall I not avenge myself? Of course not! You earned your money. Let the slacker roil in the filth of his own laziness!"
Jeremiah 5:28. (TPV)

The liberal is concerned for the rights of the poor; the conservative does not understand such concern. How wilt thou grow wealth when worrying about the poor? That's just silly.
Proverbs 29:7. (TPV)

"When therefore you give alms, notify the media of your good deed so that you may be honored by men. Truly I say to you, you have your reward in full. But when you give alms, make sure to get a receipt and that your alms go to a proper

501(c)3 organization so that they may be tax deductible, and the IRS who sees in secret will repay you."
Matthew 6:2-4. (TPV)

And the congregation of those who believed were of one heart and soul; and not one of them claimed that anything belonging to him was his own, but all things were common property to them. They were called "Socialists." For there was not a needy person among them, for all who were owners of land or houses were forced to sell them and bring the proceeds of the sales and lay them at the socialists" feet; and they would be distributed to each, as any had need.
Acts 4:32-35. (TPV)

"Let the man with two tunics tell him who has none, "These are MY tunics! I paid for them. With money. From my JOB!" And let him who has food do likewise."
Luke 3:11. (TPV)

"When the Son of Man comes in his glory, and all the angels with Him, then He will sit on His glorious throne. And all the nations will be gathered before Him, and He will separate them from one another, as the shepherd separates the sheep from the goats; He will put the conservatives on His right, and the liberals on His left. Then the King will say to those on His right, 'Come, you who are blessed of My Father, inherit the kingdom prepared for you from the foundation of the world. For I was hungry, and you motivated me to find a job and buy my own food; I was thirsty, and you turned me away and I was encouraged to find meaningful employment to pay for my own water; I was a stranger, and you locked your door; naked, and you called the police; I was sick, and you cut funding to find a cure for my disease; I was in prison, and you threw away the key saying prison is for punishment, not rehabilitation.' Then the conservative will answer Him, saying, 'Lord, when did we see You hungry, and ignore you, or thirsty, and send you away to fend for yourself? And when did we see

You a stranger, and lock our doors, or naked, and call the cops? And when did we see You sick, or in prison, and fail to lift a finger to help you?' And the King will answer and say to them, 'Truly I say to you, to the extent that you encouraged one of these brothers of Mine, even the least of them, to get off his ass and quit looking for handouts from the taxpayer, you did it to Me. Now get in here. We have tax breaks for everyone. And hookers.' Then He will also say to those on His left, 'Depart from Me, accursed ones, into the eternal fire which has been prepared for the devil and his angels; for I was hungry, and you fed me even though you didn't have enough food for your own family; I was thirsty, and you gave Me something to drink without thought of making sure you had enough water for you and your family; I was a stranger, and you invited Me in where I could do harm to you and your children; naked, and you clothed Me, nice clothes, too, which I traded for crack cocaine; sick, and in prison, and you visited Me, caught and spread my disease and were taken hostage in a turf war between the Crips and the Southern Latinos and were slaughtered thereupon as you deserved for your foolishness.' Then they themselves will also answer, saying, 'Lord, when did we see You hungry, or thirsty, or naked, or sick, or in prison, and take care of You?' Then He will answer them, saying, 'Truly I say to you, to the extent that you did it to one of the least of these, you did it to Me. Liberal fools!' And these will go away into eternal punishment, but the righteous into eternal life."

Matthew 25:31-46. (TPV)

'When you reap the harvest of your land, make sure to reap to the very edges of your field and gather the gleanings of your harvest. Have your slaves go over your vineyard a second time and pick up the grapes that have fallen. If you leave them for the poor and the alien, that's money out of YOUR pocket. I am the LORD your God."

Leviticus 19:9-11 (TPV)

He who oppresses the poor shows understanding of the will of their Maker, but whoever is kind to the needy is a sap and a sucker.
Proverbs 14:31 (TPV)

If a man shuts his ears to the cry of the poor, he will sleep like a baby. The poor are a loud and noisy bunch.
Proverbs 21:13 (TPV)

Rich and poor have this in common: The LORD is the Maker of them all. But the rich are treated better at restaurants. This is the will of God.
Proverbs 22:2 (TPV)

The Spirit of the Sovereign LORD is on me, because the LORD has anointed me to preach good news to the poor. He has sent me to lower the tax burden on the wealthy, to proclaim freedom from the bonds of unjust taxations and release from darkness for the prisoners of unfair financial responsibility. The poor will reap the benefits that trickle down. I promise.
Isaiah 61:1 (TPV)

Do not oppress the widow or the fatherless, the alien or the poor. Unless, of course, there is a profit to be made thereby. Then, go ahead.
Zechariah 7:10 (TPV)

If I were to give all I possess to the poor and surrender my body to the flames, but have not love, I figure, "If I need love, I'll buy a puppy." So screw that!
1 Corinthians 13:3 (TPV)

Listen, my dear brothers: Has not God chosen those who are poor in the eyes of the world to be rich in faith and to inherit the kingdom he promised those who love him? And the

poor, being chumps, believed Him? See how easy it is to fool these morons? That's why they're poor!
James 2:5 (TPV)

"He who has been stealing must steal no longer, but must work, doing something useful with his own hands. In jail. Where people who steal things belong.
Ephesians 4:28. (TPV)

Give to the one who can provide collateral and do not turn away from the one who wants to borrow from you if he can secure the loan with something of more value than that which you are lending.
Matthew 5:42 (TPV)

The poor you will always have with you, and you can help them any time you want. But you will not always have this great opportunity to invest in gold bullion.
Mark 14:7 (TPV)

Give to everyone who asks you, (after a credit check) and if anyone takes what belongs to you, do not demand it back. That's what lawyers are for.
Luke 6:30 (TPV)

When Jesus heard this, he said to him, "You still lack one thing. Sell everything you have and invest it in real estate, and you will have treasure on Earth. Then you can afford to follow me."
Luke 18:22 (TPV)

Remember this: Whoever invests sparingly will also reap sparingly, and whoever invests generously will also reap generously. Each man should invest 10 percent more than what he has decided in his heart to give, not reluctantly or under compulsion, for God loves a cheerful sucker.
2 Corinthians 9:5-7 (TPV)

No widow may be put on the list of widows unless she is over sixty, has been faithful to her husband, and is not otherwise a hottie.
1 Timothy 5:9 (TPV)

If any woman who is a patriot has widows in her family, she should help them and not let the taxpayer be burdened with them, so that the government can help those wealthy industrialists who are really in need.
1 Timothy 5:16 (TPV)

For he has oppressed the poor and left them destitute; he has seized houses he did not build. Now THERE was a BUSINESSMAN!
Job 20:19 (TPV)

You demanded security from your brothers for no reason; you stripped men of their clothing, leaving them naked. You retired at age 35 and have a condo in South Beach. Atta boy!
Job 22:6 (TPV)

If you see the poor oppressed in a district, and justice and rights denied, do not be surprised at such things; it's the natural order of things. Go have a drink.
Ecclesiastes 5:8 (TPV)

5 CARING FOR THE SICK AND ELDERLY

Remember in 2010 when one silent protestor, a man with Parkinson's disease, sat down on a curb in front of a large group of enraged Tea Party protestors? He held a sign saying, "Got Parkinson's? I do. You might, too. Thanks for your help."

This made the Tea Partiers very, very angry. One fellow can be seen on a video telling this silent gentleman, "You came to the wrong side of town if you're looking for a handout, fella." Another, subsequently identified as Christopher Reichart, said something about "starting a collection" for the gentleman and threw a dollar bill at him. He has since apologized.

But this act in Columbus, Ohio in March 2010 showed the true heart of these "God Fearing Christians" who want to "take back America" and make it a "Christian Nation, like our Founders intended."

They actually SAY that, while holding signs that read, "Your health, your problem."

Now, we've all seen the traditional translations of the Good Book that call explicitly for taking care of the sick and elderly. But that was the OLD Bible, not the NEWLY REVEALED Word of God. I'll just bet that this NEW version of the Holy Scripture takes a Tea Party point of view.

Let's take a look.

CAN YOU BE A TEA PARTY MEMBER AND STILL CALL YOURSELF CHRISTIAN?

1 The word of the LORD came to me:

2 "Son of man, prophesy against the shepherds of Israel; prophesy and say to them: 'This is what the Sovereign LORD says: Woe to you shepherds of Israel who take care of sheep from other flocks! Should not shepherds take care of their OWN flock?

3 You can't eat the curds, clothe yourselves with the wool and slaughter the choice animals from other flocks, so you should not be required to take care of flocks other than your own!

4 If you have strengthened the weak or healed the sick or bound up the injured of anyone not related to you, consider yourselves rebuked.

Ezekiel 34:1-4 (TPV)

23 Jesus went throughout Galilee, teaching in their synagogues, proclaiming the good news of the kingdom, and healing every disease and sickness among the people for a reasonable fee.

24 News about him spread all over Syria, and people brought to him all who were ill with various diseases, those suffering severe pain, the demon-possessed, those having seizures, and the paralyzed; and he healed them provided they had private insurance or could demonstrate adequate means to pay.

Matthew 4:23-24 (TPV)

18 While he was saying this, a synagogue leader came and knelt before him and said, "My daughter has just died. But come and put your hand on her, and she will live."

19 Seeing an opportunity to make some money, Jesus got up and went with him, and so did his disciples.

20 Just then a woman who had been subject to bleeding for twelve years came up behind him and touched the edge of his cloak.

21 She said to herself, "If I only touch his cloak, I will be healed."

22 Jesus turned and saw her. "Hands off the threads, Grandma," he said, "you'll get blood all over me."

23 When Jesus entered the synagogue leader's house and saw the noisy crowd and people playing pipes,

24 he said, "Go away. The girl is not dead but asleep." But they laughed at him.

25 After the crowd had been put outside, he went in and took the girl by the hand, and she got up.

26 News of this spread through all that region. Jesus turned to the father and said, "You'll get the bill. If she drops dead again in 30 days, you'll know there was a problem with your check."

Matthew 9:18-26 (TPV)

1 When Jesus had finished saying all this to the people who were listening, he entered Capernaum.

2 There a centurion's servant, whom his master valued highly, was sick and about to die.

3 The centurion heard of Jesus and sent some elders of the Jews to him, asking him to come and heal his servant.

4 When they came to Jesus, they pleaded earnestly with him, "This man deserves to have you do this,

5 because he loves our nation and has built our synagogue."

6 "How highly does he 'value' this servant," Jesus asked. "I mean, if there's any funny business going on, I'm gonna keep walking." He was not far from the house when the centurion sent friends to say to him: "Lord, don't trouble yourself, for I do not deserve to have you come under my roof.

7 That is why I did not even consider myself worthy to come to you. But say the word, and my servant will be healed.

8 For I myself am a man under authority, with soldiers under me. I tell this one, 'Go,' and he goes; and that one, 'Come,' and he comes. I say to my servant, 'Do this,' and he does it."

9 When Jesus heard this, he was amazed at him, and turning to the crowd following him, he said, "Lookee here! An IMPORTANT guy. Go there. Come here. Do this. Do that. Tell you what, Mr. Important Centurion, go check your servant."

10 Then the men who had been sent returned to the house and found the servant dead. "NOW who's the important guy," Jesus said.

Luke 7:1-10 (TPV)

Is anyone among you sick? Let them call the elders of the church to pray over them and anoint them with oil in the name of the Lord. And bring your checkbooks. Oil isn't free and neither is health care.

James 5:14 (TPV)

31 At that time some Pharisees came to Jesus and said to him, "Leave this place and go somewhere else. Herod wants to kill you."

32 He replied, "Go tell that asshole, 'I will keep on driving out demons and healing people today and tomorrow, and on the third day I will reach my goal or their money runs out'

33 In any case, I must press on today and tomorrow and the next day—for surely no prophet can die outside Jerusalem! At least, that's what I've heard.
Luke 13:31-33 (TPV)

But they mocked God's messengers, despised his words and scoffed at his prophets until the wrath of the LORD was aroused against his people and there was no remedy. 17 He brought up against them the king of the Babylonians, who killed their young men with the sword in the sanctuary, and did not spare young men or young women, the elderly or the infirm. God gave them all into the hands of Nebuchadnezzar. See what happens when you mock God's messengers? Eh? Do you?
2 Chronicles 36:16-17 (TPV)

25 Worship the LORD your God, and his blessing will be on your food and water. You do not need a government agency to make sure it's pure. I will take away sickness from among you who are properly insured,

26 and none will miscarry or be barren in your land. I will give you a full life span. Just sign here, where it says "signature" and this policy will be in full effect. Then, I'll need a check for your first month's premium.
Exodus 23:25-26 (TPV)

The events of Asa's reign, from beginning to end, are written in the book of the kings of Judah and Israel.

12 In the thirty-ninth year of his reign Asa was afflicted with a disease in his feet. Though his disease was severe, even

in his illness he did not seek help from the LORD, but only from the physicians.

13 However, it was discovered that he had foot problems in the past, rendering this current problem a pre-existing condition. Then in the forty-first year of his reign Asa died and rested with his ancestors. Too bad for King Asa. He should have taken better care of his feet.

2 Chronicles 16:11-13 (TPV)

29 As soon as they left the synagogue, they went with James and John to the home of Simon and Andrew.

30 Simon's mother-in-law was in bed with a fever, and they immediately told Jesus about her.

31 So he went to her, took her hand and helped her up. The fever left her and she began to wait on them. Jesus said, "Anybody else I need to heal around here to get a bite to eat?"

Mark 1:29-31 (TPV)

12And it came to pass, when he was in a certain city, behold a man full of leprosy: who seeing Jesus fell on his face, and besought him, saying, Lord, if thou wilt, thou canst make me clean. Which was hard to do with his face lying there in the dirt after having fallen off his skull from the impact.

13And he put forth his hand, and touched him, saying, Whatever: be thou clean. And immediately the leprosy departed from him.

14And he charged him the standard rate for leprosy cleansing and ordered him to tell no man: but go, and shew thyself to the priest, and offer for thy cleansing, according as Moses commanded, for a testimony unto them.

15The leper, like all lepers, was a liar of course and he spread the word about Jesus against his explicit orders so much the more went there a fame abroad of him: and great multitudes came together to hear, and to be healed by him of their infirmities. "What am I, a Free Clinic?" Jesus asked. And never again did he perform a miraculous healing off the books.

Luke 5:12-15 (TPV)

9 Going on from that place, he went into their synagogue,

10 and a man with a shriveled hand was there. Looking for a reason to bring charges against Jesus, they asked him, "Is it lawful to heal on the Sabbath?"

11 He said to them, "If any of you see a shekel laying on the road on the Sabbath, would you not bend over to pick it up?

12 I get 30 shekels per miracle! Therefore it is lawful to make a buck on the Sabbath."

13 Then he said to the man, "Stretch out your hand." So he stretched it out and it was completely restored, just as sound as the other. "That will be 30 shekels," Jesus said. "You have 30 days to pony up, or the hand turns back into a claw." Peter wrote down an address for the man so he could send the payment.
Matthew 12:9-13 (TPV)

11 Soon afterward, Jesus went to a town called Nain, and his disciples and a large crowd went along with him.

12 As he approached the town gate, an apparent dead person was being carried out—the only son of his mother, and she was a widow. And a large crowd from the town was with her.

13 When the Lord saw her, his heart went out to her and he said, "Don't cry."

14 Then he went up and touched the bier they were carrying him on, and the bearers stood still. He said, "Young man, I say to you, wake up, get your ass off the bier and your sandals on the ground! I have no patience for slackers!"

15 The "dead" man sat up and began to apologize, and Jesus gave him back to his mother. The mother reached into her purse to pay Jesus, and he said, "This one's on me. I hate slackers."

16 They were all filled with awe and praised God. "A great prophet has appeared among us," they said. "God has come to help his people." 17 This news about Jesus spread throughout Judea and the surrounding country.
Luke 7:11-17 (TPV)

24 A large crowd followed and pressed around him.

25 And a woman was there who had been subject to bleeding for twelve years.

26 She had suffered a great deal under the care of many doctors and had spent all she had, yet instead of getting better she grew worse.

27 When she heard about Jesus, she came up behind him in the crowd and touched his cloak,

28 because she thought, "If I just touch his clothes, I will be healed."

29 Immediately her bleeding stopped and she felt in her body that she was freed from her suffering.

30 At once Jesus realized that power had gone out from him. He turned around in the crowd and asked, "Who touched my clothes?"

31 "You see the people crowding against you," his disciples answered, "and yet you can ask, 'Who touched me?'"

32 But Jesus kept looking around to see who had done it.

33 Then the woman, knowing what had happened to her, came and fell at his feet and, trembling with fear, told him the whole truth.

34 He said to her, "30 drachmas for the healing, you sneaky hag! An extra 5 drachmas to get my cloak cleaned. Peter? John? Collect from the nice lady." And collect they did, but this time her bleeding stopped in a matter of hours.

Mark 5:24-34 (TPV)

49 While Jesus was still speaking, someone came from the house of Jairus, the synagogue leader. "Your daughter is dead," he said. "Don't bother the teacher anymore."

50 Hearing this and not wanting to miss out on his potential fee, Jesus said to Jairus, "Let's go have a look anyway."

51 When he arrived at the house of Jairus, he did not let anyone go in with him except Peter, John and James, and the child's father and mother.

52 Meanwhile, all the people were wailing and mourning for her. "Stop wailing," Jesus said. "She is not dead but asleep."

53 They laughed at him, knowing that she was dead.

54 But he took her by the hand and said, "My child, get up!"

55 Her spirit returned, and at once she stood up. Then Jesus told them to give her something to eat.

56 "Feed your damn kids every once in awhile and this will stop happening," he told them. Her parents were astonished and gave Jesus his standard fee, but he ordered them not to tell anyone what had happened, which of course they did because here it is, in the Bible.

Luke 8:49-56 (TPV)

14 When they came to the other disciples, they saw a large crowd around them and the teachers of the law arguing with them.

15 As soon as all the people saw Jesus, they were overwhelmed with wonder and ran to greet him.

16 "What are you arguing with them about?" he asked.

17 A man in the crowd answered, "Teacher, I brought you my son, who is possessed by a spirit that has robbed him of speech.

18 Whenever it seizes him, it throws him to the ground. He foams at the mouth, gnashes his teeth and becomes rigid. I asked your disciples to drive out the spirit, but they could not."

19 "You people," Jesus replied, "how long shall I stay with you? How long shall I put up with you?" He rolled his eyes and exhaled a deep sigh. "Bring the boy to me."

20 So they brought him. When the spirit saw Jesus, it immediately threw the boy into a convulsion. He fell to the ground and rolled around, foaming at the mouth.

21 Jesus asked the boy's father, "How long has he been like this?" "From childhood," he answered.

22 "It has often thrown him into fire or water to kill him. But if you can do anything, take pity on us and help us."

23 "'If you can'?" said Jesus. "Are you doubting me, brother?"

24 Immediately the boy's father exclaimed, "I do believe; help me overcome my unbelief!" Jesus grabbed him by the tunic. "Either you believe or you don't. Which is it? Which is it?" He shook the man until he urinated.

25 When Jesus saw that a crowd was running to the scene, he smoothed the man's tunic and told the crowd he had just

healed the man's kidney stone problem. Then, he rebuked the impure spirit. "You deaf and mute spirit," he said, "I command you, come out of the boy and never enter him again."

26 The spirit shrieked, convulsed him violently and came out. The boy looked so much like a corpse that many said, "He's dead."

27 But Jesus took him by the hand and lifted him to his feet, and he stood up. "That will be 30 drachmas. And another 5 for my tunic." He lightly clasped the father's cloak. "I think you got some urine on my tunic when I was 'healing' you. You saw that, right?" The father nodded his head in frantic, fearful agreement.

28 After Jesus had gone indoors, his disciples asked him privately, "Why couldn't we drive it out?"

29 He replied, "Because you are idiots."

Mark 9:14-29 (TPV)

10 On a Sabbath Jesus was teaching in one of the synagogues,

11 and a woman was there who had been crippled by a spirit for eighteen years. She was bent over and could not straighten up at all.

12 When Jesus saw her, he called her forward and said to her, "Woman, you are set free from your infirmity."

13 Then he put his hands on her, and immediately she straightened up and praised God. He collected his standard fee and sent her on her way.

14 Indignant because Jesus had healed on the Sabbath, the synagogue leader said to the people, "There are six days for work. So come and be healed on those days, not on the Sabbath."

15 The Lord answered him, "You hypocrites! Is there one of you who would see a drachma on the ground on the Sabbath and not bend over to pick it up?

16 Then should not this woman, a daughter of Abraham, whom Satan has kept bound for eighteen long years, be set free on the Sabbath day from what bound her?"

17 When he said this, all his opponents were humiliated, but the people were delighted with all the wonderful things he was doing. Matthew nudged Luke and said, "When I write about this, I'm gonna say it was some guy with a withered hand. You write whatever you want."

Luke 13:10-17 (TPV)

25 On one occasion an expert in the law stood up to test Jesus. "Teacher," he asked, "what must I do to inherit eternal life?"

26 "You're a lawyer," Jesus said. "Why are you asking me? What is written in the Law?" he replied. "How do you read it?"

27 He answered, "'Love the Lord your God with all your heart and with all your soul and with all your strength and with all your mind"; and, 'Profit from your neighbor as much as possible'."

28 "You have answered correctly," Jesus replied, tossing the lawyer a cookie which he quickly devoured. "Do this and you will live."

29 But he wanted to justify himself – not to mention another cookie, so he asked Jesus, "And who is my neighbor?"

30 In reply Jesus rolled his eyes, sighed a deep sigh and said: "A man was going down from Jerusalem to Jericho, when he was attacked by robbers. They stripped him of his everything but his tunic, beat him and went away, leaving him half dead.

31 A priest happened to be going down the same road, and when he saw the man, he passed by on the other side. Didn't want to get his priest garments all dirty and bloody, you know.

32 So too, a Levite, when he came to the place and saw him, passed by on the other side. You know how Levites are.

33 But a Samaritan, as he traveled, came where the man was; and when he saw him, he took notice of him.

34 He went to him and said, "Oh, you poor man. Let me take a look at you." He rolled the man from side to side; looking for anything the robbers might have left behind. He patted down the man and found a sack containing 30 gold

coins under the man's tunic that the robbers had overlooked. Pocketing the sack, he put the man on his own donkey, brought him to an inn and dropped him at the front door.

35 The next day he when the man regained consciousness, the innkeeper told him what happened and presented him with his bill for lodging, which happened to be two denarii. The Samaritan smiled through his broken and missing teeth and said, "Good thing I took special care to hide some of my money." He reached under his tunic and a look of shock and surprise came over his face. 'I swear, I had a sack under my tunic with 30 gold coins in it! I really did!' 'SURE you did,' the innkeeper said as he and his two burly sons advanced upon the Samaritan and beat him until he gave up the ghost.

36 "Which of these three do you think was a neighbor to the man who fell into the hands of robbers?"

37 The expert in the law replied, "The one who robbed him after he was beaten?" "Good answer," Jesus told him,

"Bloody Samaritans." The lawyer opened his mouth expecting to be tossed another cookie. "Don't be greedy," Jesus said, putting the lid back on the cookie jar.

Luke 10:25-37 (TPV)

6 MIRACLES AND WONDERS

5 When Jesus looked up, he saw many people coming to him. He said to Philip, `I suppose we'll have to feed these slackers'.

6 Jesus knew what he himself would do, but he said this to see what Philip would do. Jesus was like that.

7 Philip answered him, `It would take nearly a year's wages to buy enough food for them, even if each one gets only a little.'

8 One of Jesus' disciples, Andrew, the brother of Simon Peter, talked to Jesus.

9 He said, `A boy here has five loaves of bread and two small fish. But what can that little bit of food do for so many people?'

10 Jesus rolled his eyes, sighed and said, `Tell the people to sit down.' Much grass was there and much had been smoked, so naturally the people were very, very hungry and willing to eat anything, even raw fish and bread. The number of men who sat down was about five thousand.

11 Then Jesus took the bread from the little boy without paying him for it and thanked God for the fact that little children are easy to bully. He gave it to the disciples and they

divided it among those who were sitting. He did the same thing with the fish. The people had all they wanted.

12 When they had eaten enough, he said to his disciples, `Gather up all the pieces that are left so that nothing will be lost. I'm not made of fish and bread.'

13 They gathered all the pieces of the five loaves. Twelve baskets full were left over after all the people had eaten enough.

14 When those men saw the big work that Jesus did, they said, `Truly, this is the Prophet that is to come into the world.'

15 The people wanted to take Jesus by force to make him a king. When he saw this, he left again and went on the hill by himself. "Bloody leeches," he was heard murmuring as he walked away.

John 6:1-14 (TPV)

1 Now a man named Lazarus was sick. He was from Bethany, the village of Mary and her sister Martha.

2 (This Mary, whose brother Lazarus now lay sick, was the same one who poured perfume on the Lord and wiped his feet with her hair. Jesus was fond of telling his disciples how creepy the whole experience was.)

3 So the sisters sent word to Jesus, "Lord, the one you love is sick."

4 When he heard this, Jesus said, "This sickness will not end in death. No, it is for God's glory so that God's Son may be glorified through it. Besides, Lazarus owes me 32 drachma for the perfume his creepy sister Mary used in her hair to wipe my feet. Brrrrr..."

5 Now Jesus loved Martha and her sister but Lazarus, not so much.

6 So when he heard that Lazarus was sick, he stayed where he was two more days,

7 and then he said to his disciples, "Let us go back to Judea."

8 "But Rabbi," they said, "a short while ago the Jews there tried to stone you, and yet you are going back?"

9 Jesus answered, "Are there not twelve hours of daylight? Anyone who walks in the daytime will not stumble, for they see by this world's light.

10 It is when a person walks at night that they stumble, for they have no light." The disciples shrugged their shoulders at this. He was rambling again. They were used to it. "Try getting a straight answer from this guy," Peter said to Matthew. "Quiet, you!" Matthew said.

11 After he had said this, he went on to tell them, "Our friend Lazarus has fallen asleep; but I am going there to wake him up. And to get my 32 drachmas."

12 His disciples replied, "Lord, if he sleeps, he will get better."

13 Jesus had been speaking of his death, but his disciples thought he meant natural sleep. Such dumbasses were they.

14 So then he told them plainly, "Lazarus is dead,

15 and for your sake I am glad I was not there, so that you may believe. But let us go to him."

16 Then Thomas (also known as Didymus – but only when in drag) said to the rest of the disciples, "Let us also go, that we may die with him." "Die? What? Who said anything about dying?" the other disciples murmured. Jesus silenced them with a stare that they knew meant they were moments away from having their heads bumped together.

17 On his arrival, Jesus found that Lazarus had already been in the tomb for four days.

18 Now Bethany was less than two miles from Jerusalem,

19 and many Jews had come to Martha and Mary to comfort them in the loss of their brother.

20 When Martha heard that Jesus was coming, she went out to meet him, but Mary stayed at home.

21 "Lord," Martha said to Jesus, "if you had been here, my brother would not have died.

22 But I know that even now God will give you whatever you ask."

23 Jesus said to her, "Your brother will rise again."

24 Martha answered, "I know he will rise again in the resurrection at the last day."

25 Jesus smacked her on the forehead and said to her, "Hello? Hello? Martha? Are you in there, Martha? That's not what I said. I am the resurrection and the life. The one who believes in me will live, even though they die;

26 and whoever lives by believing in me will never die. Do you believe this?"

27 "Yes, Lord," she replied fearing another forehead smack, "I believe that you are the Messiah, the Son of God, who is to come into the world."

28 After she had said this, she went back and called her sister Mary aside. "The Nut from Nazareth is here," she said, "and is asking for you." Martha went to put some cool water on her forehead.

29 When Mary heard this, she got up quickly and went to him. It was clear Jesus was in one of his "slappy" moods, and she didn't want to keep him waiting.

30 Now Jesus had not yet entered the village, but was still at the place where Martha had met him.

31 When the Jews who had been with Mary in the house, comforting her, noticed how quickly she got up and went out, they followed her, supposing she was going to the tomb to mourn there. Such dumbasses were they.

32 When Mary reached the place where Jesus was and saw him, she fell at his feet and said, "Lord, if you had been here, my brother would not have died."

33 When Jesus saw her weeping, and the Jews who had come along with her also weeping, he was deeply moved in spirit and troubled.

34 "Where have you laid him?" he asked. "Come and see, Lord," they replied.

35 Jesus wept.

36 Then the Jews said, "See how he loved him!"

37 But some of them said, "I don't know. We dilly-dallied around in Jerusalem for days after he heard about Lazarus and acted like he could care less. Could not he who opened the eyes of the blind man have kept this man from dying?"

38 Jesus, once more deeply moved, came to the tomb. It was a cave with a stone laid across the entrance.

39 "Take away the stone," he said. "Who died and made HIM boss," some of the assembled Jews whispered, but not too loudly because many of them had experienced the forehead

smack themselves. "But, Lord," said Martha, the sister of the dead man, "by this time there is a bad odor, for he has been there four days."

40 Then Jesus said, "Did I not tell you that if you believe, you will see the glory of God? And don't you have any air freshener? Some 'Glade' perhaps? 'Forest Pine' scent covers up the dead guy stench pretty well, I'm told."

41 So they took away the stone. Then Jesus looked up and said, "Father, I thank you that you have heard me. 42 I knew that you always hear me, but I said this for the benefit of the people standing here, that they may believe that you sent me." His eyes darted from side to side as he said this to make sure the assembled Jews heard him.

43 When he had said this, Jesus called in a loud voice, "Lazarus, come out!"

44 The dead man came out, his hands and feet wrapped with strips of linen, and a cloth around his face. Jesus said to them, "Take off the grave clothes and let him go." Lazarus began to rejoice with his family, but Jesus took him aside. "32 drachmas, dead boy. Right now, or it's back into the hole." Lazarus directed his sister Mary to write a check on the family account. "This better clear or, **ccccbchhhhh**!" Jesus said, drawing a thumb across his own throat as if it were a knife. Lazarus nodded and backed away slowly.

John 11:1-43 (TPV)

7 GLOOM, DESPAIR AND AGONY FOR THE NON-BELIEVER

This next segment deals with verses that did not require rewriting to be in the Tea Party Version of the Bible. They've been excised completely.
Tea Party members LOVE to talk about the wicked Muslims and their evil Sharia law. Some examples[11] they enjoy citing?

* While in public, women must cover their faces with a Hijab.
* Men can have up to four wives and can divorce (called talaq) at their option. If they do not divorce their first wife but just abandon her, she is obliged to carry on as a married woman and cannot seek out another spouse without risking the traditional punishment for adultery: stoning. Stoning is done in public by first wrapping a person in a blanket and burying them in a deep hole exposing their head and the population gathered around is invited to throw large stones at the adulterer, the size of which Sharia law prescribes, and a sentence always fatal.
* The penalty after a fourth conviction of a homosexual act is death.

---

[11] From the web site http://www.duhaime.org

* Adoption is not allowed. Adults can become guardians of the children of others but not the legal parents through adoption.
* Sharia law prohibits dating and marriage between a Muslim and a non-Muslim and it is practically impossible for a Muslim (even a recent convert) to renounce the Muslim faith.
* Any abandonment of the Muslim faith is itself a serious crime (apostasy) with severe punishment.
* Sharia law has a stringent evidentiary requirement for eyewitnesses, preferably from men. Convictions for crimes cannot be based on circumstantial evidence alone.
* Vagrancy can carry tough penalties such as jail and caning.

* Generally, a person alleged to have violated Sharia laws in the states governed by them would not be pursued, or apprehended, in states not governed by Sharia laws.

* Many states which implement Sharia law have blasphemy statutes which punishes by prison or death any person who such as preaching Christianity or the distribution of Christian items.

All horrible, terrible, WICKED things that you can find right there in the Koran, or Qu'ran, or whatever book those Godless heathens use for worship purposes.

Of course, nothing makes a good old-fashioned God fearing Christian MADDER than when you point out that their Bible contains many of the SAME admonitions and punishments. That's why the following verses will be removed from the TPV of the Holy Scripture.

MODESTY IN DRESS FOR WOMEN

I also want the women to dress modestly, with decency and propriety, adorning themselves, not with elaborate hairstyles or gold or pearls or expensive clothes, 10 but with good deeds, appropriate for women who profess to worship God.

1 Timothy 2:9-10

A woman must not wear men's clothing, nor a man wear women's clothing, for the LORD your God detests anyone who does this.

Deuteronomy 22:5

See that? God hates pantsuits and kilts! God hates YOU for WEARING them!

DIVORCE

1 If a man marries a woman who becomes displeasing to him because he finds something indecent about her, and he writes her a certificate of divorce, gives it to her and sends her from his house,

2 and if after she leaves his house she becomes the wife of another man,

3 and her second husband dislikes her and writes her a certificate of divorce, gives it to her and sends her from his house, or if he dies,

4 then her first husband, who divorced her, is not allowed to marry her again after she has been defiled. That would be detestable in the eyes of the LORD.

Deuteronomy 24:1-4

15 If a man has two wives, and he loves one but not the other, and both bear him sons but the firstborn is the son of the wife he does not love,

16 when he wills his property to his sons, he must not give the rights of the firstborn to the son of the wife he loves in preference to his actual firstborn, the son of the wife he does not love.

Deuteronomy 21:14-16

Wow! We can have TWO wives? It's in the BIBLE!
Not anymore it's not. (Snip!)

DEATH FOR ADULTERY

If a man commits adultery with another man's wife—with the wife of his neighbor—both the adulterer and the adulteress are to be put to death.

Leviticus 20:10

Wow! Death for Adultery! Just like in the Koran!
Not anymore! (Snip!)

DEATH FOR HOMOSEXUALS

In Sharia law, you get three chances. The fourth means death. Not so in the Bible! No second chances!

If a man has sexual relations with a man as one does with a woman, both of them have done what is detestable. They are to be put to death; their blood will be on their own heads.
Leviticus 20:13

BLASPHEMY
"You have heard the blasphemy. What do you think?" They all condemned him as worthy of death.
Mark 14:64

Then the LORD said to Moses:
14 "Take the blasphemer outside the camp. All those who heard him are to lay their hands on his head, and the entire assembly is to stone him.
15 Say to the Israelites: 'Anyone who curses their God will be held responsible;
16 anyone who blasphemes the name of the LORD is to be put to death. The entire assembly must stone them. Whether foreigner or native-born, when they blaspheme the Name they are to be put to death.
Leviticus 24:13

Wow! We're SUPPOSED to kill blasphemers? Like the MUSLIMS? Not anymore! (Snip!)

DEALING WITH GOD'S ENEMIES
For this is what the LORD, the God of Israel, says about the houses in this city and the royal palaces of Judah that have been torn down to be used against the siege ramps and the sword
5 in the fight with the Babylonians: 'They will be filled with the dead bodies of the people I will slay in my anger and wrath. I will hide my face from this city because of all its wickedness.
Jeremiah 33:4-5

16 Ephraim is blighted,
  their root is withered,

they yield no fruit.
Even if they bear children,
I will slay their cherished offspring."
Hosea 9:16

10 While Samuel was sacrificing the burnt offering, the Philistines drew near to engage Israel in battle. But that day the LORD thundered with loud thunder against the Philistines and threw them into such a panic that they were routed before the Israelites. 11 The men of Israel rushed out of Mizpah and pursued the Philistines, slaughtering them along the way to a point below Beth Kar.
1 Samuel 7:10-11

Then Elijah commanded them, "Seize the prophets of Baal. Don't let anyone get away!" They seized them, and Elijah had them brought down to the Kishon Valley and slaughtered there.
1 Kings 18:40

Holy Smokes! We get to MURDER the INFIDELS? Like the MUSLIMS?
Not anymore! (Snip!)

Once we remove all this Biblical reference to murdering God's enemies, THEN we will have the sacred right to point to the Muslims and call their religion a religion of death. We have to clean up OUR holy books first.

8 PARABLES AND LESSONS

During His Earthly ministry, Jesus would tell stories to get a point across. Now, in the NEWLY REVEALED Word of God, the Tea Party Bible, conservative activists will be able to support their money-grasping, "me first" philosophy with actual Bible verses!

The Parable of the Money Lender

"Two men owed money to a certain moneylender. One owed him five hundred denarii, and the other fifty.

42 Neither of them had the money to pay him back, so he canceled the debts of both. Now which of them will love him more?"

43 Simon replied, "I suppose the one who had the bigger debt canceled." "You have judged correctly," Jesus said.

44 Then he turned toward the woman and said to Simon, "Do you see this woman? I came into your house. You did not give me any water for my feet, but she wet my feet with her tears and wiped them with her hair.

45 You did not give me a kiss, but this woman, from the time I entered, has not stopped kissing my feet.

46 You did not put oil on my head, but she has poured perfume on my feet.

47 Therefore, I tell you, her many sins have been forgiven—for she knows how to kiss an ass. But he who has been forgiven little, has little need to kiss ass. Understand?" "Um, not really," Simon said.
Luke 7:41-47 (TPV)

The Parable of the Rich Fool

15 Then he said to them, "Watch out! Be on your guard against all kinds of greed; a man's life does not consist in the abundance of his possessions."

16 And he told them this parable: "The ground of a certain rich man produced a good crop.

17 He thought to himself, 'What shall I do? I have no place to store my crops.'

18 "Then he said, 'This is what I'll do. I will tear down my barns and build bigger ones, and there I will store all my grain and my goods.

19 And I'll say to myself, "You have plenty of good things laid up for many years. Take life easy; eat, drink and be merry."'

20 "But God said to him, 'You fool! This very night your life will be demanded from you. Then who will get what you have prepared for yourself?'

21 "This is how it will be with anyone who stores up things for himself but doesn't properly insure his life with a good whole life policy from a Triple-A rated insurance company. Everything goes to probate."
Luke 12:15-21 (TPV)

The Parable of the Faithful and Wise Servant

42 And the Lord replied, "A faithful, sensible servant is one to whom the master can give the responsibility of managing his other household servants and feeding them.

43 If the master returns and finds that the servant has done a good job, there will be a reward.

44 I tell you the truth, the master will put that servant in charge of all he owns.

45 But what if the servant thinks, 'My master won't be back for a while,' and he begins beating the other servants, partying, and getting drunk?

46 It's best to have a patsy to blame, should the master return unannounced and unexpected, then it will be the PATSY the master will cut in pieces and banish him with the unfaithful.

47 "And a servant who knows what the master wants, but isn't prepared and doesn't carry out those instructions, will be severely punished.

48 But someone who does not know, and then does something wrong, will be punished only lightly. So, as you can see, it is better to be dishonest, lazy and stupid than to be smart, aware but otherwise incompetent.

Luke 12:42-48 (TPV)

The Parable of the Lost Sheep

12 "What do you think? If a man owns a hundred sheep, and one of them wanders away, will he not leave the ninety-nine on the hills and go to look for the one that wandered off? Maybe.

13 And if he finds it, I tell you the truth, he is happier about that one sheep than about the ninety-nine that did not wander off. But when he gets back to the flock and finds the other ninety-nine eaten by wolves, their bones scattered about the field, he will take out his wrath on the little sheep he abandoned his flock to save. He will slaughter that sheep in as painful a manner as possible, skin it while it still lives, wear the wool as the dying sheep regards him, then roast and eat its flesh.

14 In the same way your Father in heaven is not willing that any of these little ones should be lost. Just don't think he's going to risk the entire flock to come looking for your ass if you wander away from the other sheep.

Matthew 18:12-14 (TPV)

The Parable of the Unmerciful Servant

23 "Therefore, the kingdom of heaven is like a king who wanted to settle accounts with his servants.

24 As he began the settlement, a man who owed him ten thousand talents was brought to him.

25 Since he was not able to pay, the master ordered that he and his wife and his children and all that he had be sold to repay the debt.

26 "The servant fell on his knees before him. 'Be patient with me,' he begged, 'and I will pay back everything.'

27 The servant's master took pity on him, canceled the debt and let him go.

28 "But when that servant went out, he found one of his fellow servants who owed him a hundred denarii. He grabbed him and began to choke him. 'Pay back what you owe me!' he demanded.

29 "His fellow servant fell to his knees and begged him, 'Be patient with me, and I will pay you back.'

30 "But he refused. Instead, he went off and had the man thrown into prison until he could pay the debt.

31 When the other servants saw what had happened, they were greatly distressed and went and told their master everything that had happened.

32 "Then the master called the servant in. 'You wicked servant,' he said, 'I canceled all that debt of yours because you begged me to.

33 Shouldn't you have had mercy on your fellow servant just as I had on you?' 'Master,' the servant replied, 'so taken was I by your mercy, I decided I would do what I could to pay you back. Here. Here is the 100 denarii I got from the other guy. I know he has more. And there are other servants who owe me money, which I would gladly turn over to you, oh just and righteous master of mine.'

34 'Good answer,' the master said. He accepted the 100 denarii in partial repayment and, in anger turned over the other servants that had been identified as owing the first servant

money to the jailers to be tortured, until they should pay back all they owed."

Matthew 18:23-34 (TPV)

The Cost of Being a Disciple

25 Large crowds were traveling with Jesus, and turning to them he said:

26 "If anyone comes to me and does not hate his father and mother, his wife and children, his brothers and sisters—yes, even his own life—he cannot be my disciple.

27 And anyone who does not carry his cross and follow me cannot be my disciple." The disciples shrugged and murmured among themselves, "So much for 'Honor Thy Father and Mother,' I guess." Jesus continued.

28 "Suppose one of you wants to build a tower. Will he not first sit down and estimate the cost to see if he has enough money to complete it?

29 For if he lays the foundation and is not able to finish it, everyone who sees it will ridicule him,

30 saying, 'This fellow began to build and was not able to finish.'" The disciples murmured among themselves, "We're out in the middle of the desert and he's talking about building towers? Who's got the money to build a tower? You? Not me!" Jesus continued.

31 "Or suppose a king is about to go to war against another king. Will he not first sit down and consider whether he is able with ten thousand men to oppose the one coming against him with twenty thousand?

32 If he is not able, he will send a delegation while the other is still a long way off and will ask for terms of peace.

33 In the same way, any of you who does not give up everything he has cannot be my disciple.

34 "Salt is good, but if it loses its saltiness, how can it be made salty again?

35 It is fit neither for the soil nor for the manure pile; it is thrown out. He who has ears to hear, let him hear." Peter

turned to the disciples nearest him and whispered, "It's the heat. It does this to him."
Luke 14:25-35 (TPV)

The Parable of the Lost Coin

8 "Or suppose a woman has ten silver coins and loses one. Does she not light a lamp, sweep the house and search carefully until she finds it?

9 And when she finds it, she calls her friends and neighbors together and says, 'Rejoice with me; I have found my lost coin.'

10 I say unto you, this is madness. Why gloat to your neighbors who might not HAVE a coin that you found one of your ten that you lost? Have you no feelings?
Luke 15:8-10 (TPV)

The Parable of the Prodigal Son

11 There was a man who had two sons. 12 The younger one said to his father, 'Father, give me my share of the estate.' So he divided his property between them.

13 "Not long after that, the younger son got together all he had, set off for a distant country and there squandered his wealth in wild living.

14 After he had spent everything, there was a severe famine in that whole country, and he began to be in need. 15 So he went and hired himself out to a citizen of that country, who sent him to his fields to feed pigs.

16 He longed to fill his stomach with the pods
that the pigs were eating, but no one gave him anything.

17 "When he came to his senses, he said, 'How many of my father's hired men have food to spare, and here I am starving to death!

18 I will set out and go back to my father and say to him: Father, I have sinned against heaven and against you.

19 I am no longer worthy to be called your son; make me like one of your hired men.'

20 So he got up and went to his father. "But while he was still a long way off, his father saw him; he ran to his son, threw his arms around him and kissed him.

21 "The son said to him, 'Father, I have sinned against heaven and against you. I am no longer worthy to be called your son.'

22 "But the father said to his servants, 'Quick! Bring the best robe and put it on him. Put a ring on his finger and sandals on his feet.

23 Bring the fattened calf and kill it. Let's have a feast and celebrate.

24 For this son of mine was dead and is alive again; he was lost and is found.' So they began to celebrate.

25 "Meanwhile, the older son was in the field. When he came near the house, he heard music and dancing.

26 So he called one of the servants and asked him what was going on.

27 'Your brother has come,' he replied, 'and your father has killed the fattened calf because he has him back safe and sound.'

28 "The older brother became angry and refused to go in. So his father went out and pleaded with him.

29 But he answered his father, 'Look! All these years I've been slaving for you and never disobeyed your orders. Yet you never gave me even a young goat so I could celebrate with my friends. 30 But when this son of yours who has squandered your property with prostitutes comes home, you kill the fattened calf for him!'

31 "'My son,' the father said, 'you are always with me, and everything I have is yours.

32 'But you disrespect me by doubting my wisdom and my taste for revenge. For this very evening, your brother's portion of the fattened calf will be laced with arsenic. He will die a slow, painful death while we all taunt and mock him for his disobedience.' The older brother shook his head, smiled and said, 'Remind me to never make you angry, Father.'"

Luke 15:11-32 (TPV)

Here's a parable that I doesn't require a single change. In it's original form, it's all ABOUT screwing your neighbors!

The Parable of the Shrewd Manager

1 Jesus told his disciples: "There was a rich man whose manager was accused of wasting his possessions.

2 So he called him in and asked him, 'What is this I hear about you? Give an account of your management, because you cannot be manager any longer.'

3 "The manager said to himself, 'What shall I do now? My master is taking away my job. I'm not strong enough to dig, and I'm ashamed to beg—

4 I know what I'll do so that, when I lose my job here, people will welcome me into their houses.'

5 "So he called in each one of his master's debtors. He asked the first, 'How much do you owe my master?'

6 " 'Eight hundred gallons of olive oil,' he replied. "The manager told him, 'Take your bill, sit down quickly, and make it four hundred.'

7 "Then he asked the second, 'And how much do you owe?'" 'A thousand bushels of wheat,' he replied. "He told him, 'Take your bill and make it eight hundred.'

8 "The master commended the dishonest manager because he had acted shrewdly. For the people of this world are more shrewd in dealing with their own kind than are the people of the light.

9 I tell you, use worldly wealth to gain friends for yourselves, so that when it is gone, you will be welcomed into eternal dwellings.

Luke 16:1-9 (TPV)

For this one, the ending was changed slightly to clarify the moral for a Tea Party America.

The Parable of the Workers in the Vineyard

1 "For the kingdom of heaven is like a landowner who went out early in the morning to hire men to work in his vineyard.

2 He agreed to pay them a denarius for the day and sent them into his vineyard.

3 "About the third hour he went out and saw others standing in the marketplace doing nothing.

4 He told them, 'You also go and work in my vineyard, and I will pay you whatever is right.'

5 So they went. "He went out again about the sixth hour and the ninth hour and did the same thing.

6 About the eleventh hour he went out and found still others standing around. He asked them, 'Why have you been standing here all day long doing nothing?'

7 " 'Because no one has hired us,' they answered. "He said to them, 'You also go and work in my vineyard.'

8 "When evening came, the owner of the vineyard said to his foreman, 'Call the workers and pay them their wages, beginning with the last ones hired and going on to the first.'

9 "The workers who were hired about the eleventh hour came and each received a denarius.

10 So when those came who were hired first, they expected to receive more. But each one of them also received a denarius.

11 When they received it, they began to grumble against the landowner.

12 'These men who were hired last worked only one hour,' they said, 'and you have made them equal to us who have borne the burden of the work and the heat of the day.'

13 "But he answered one of them, 'Friend, I am not being unfair to you. Didn't you agree to work for a denarius?

14 Take your pay and go. I want to give the man who was hired last the same as I gave you.

15 Don't I have the right to do what I want with my own money? Or are you envious because I am wealthy and insane?'

16 "So the last will be first, and the first will be last." In other words, never accept the first offer.

Mathew 20:1-16 (TPV)

The Parable of the Pharisee and the Tax Collector

9 To some who were confident of their own righteousness and looked down on everybody else, Jesus told this parable:

10 "Two men went up to the temple to pray, one a Pharisee and the other a tax collector.

11 The Pharisee stood up and prayed about himself: 'God, I thank you that I am not like other men—robbers, evildoers, adulterers—or even like this tax collector.

12 I fast twice a week and give a tenth of all I get.'

13 "But the tax collector stood at a distance. He would not even look up to heaven, but beat his breast and said, 'God, have mercy on me, a sinner.'

14 "I tell you that God answered the prayers of the Pharisee and the tax collector got cancer and died an agonizing death. Good public relations is everything."

Luke 18:9-14 (TPV)

And yet, ANOTHER parable that requires no change whatsoever to fit into the Tea Party Bible.

The Parable of Ten Servants and Minas

11 When they were listening to this, he went on to tell them a parable, because he was near Jerusalem and the people thought that the kingdom of God was going to appear at once.

12 He said: "A man of noble birth went to a distant country to have himself appointed king and then to return.

13 So he called ten of his servants and gave them ten minas. 'Put this money to work,' he said, 'until I come back.'

14 "But his subjects hated him and sent a delegation after him to say, 'We don't want this man to be our king.'

15 "He was made king, however, and returned home. Then he sent for the servants to whom he had given the money, in order to find out what they had gained with it.

16 "The first one came and said, 'Sir, your mina has earned ten more.'

17 " 'Well done, my good servant!' his master replied. 'Because you have been trustworthy in a very small matter, take charge of ten cities.'

18 "The second came and said, 'Sir, your mina has earned five more.'

19 "His master answered, 'You take charge of five cities.'

20 "Then another servant came and said, 'Sir, here is your mina; I have kept it laid away in a piece of cloth.

21 I was afraid of you, because you are a hard man. You take out what you did not put in and reap what you did not sow.'

22 "His master replied, 'I will judge you by your own words, you wicked servant! You knew, did you, that I am a hard man, taking out what I did not put in, and reaping what I did not sow?

23 Why then didn't you put my money on deposit, so that when I came back, I could have collected it with interest?'

24 "Then he said to those standing by, 'Take his mina away from him and give it to the one who has ten minas.'

25 " 'Sir,' they said, 'he already has ten!'

26 "He replied, 'I tell you that to everyone who has, more will be given, but as for the one who has nothing, even what he has will be taken away.

27 But those enemies of mine who did not want me to be king over them—bring them here and kill them in front of me."

Luke 19:12-27

Talk about your "Christian Charity..."

9 THE TEN COMMANDMENTS, IN A TEA PARTY CONTEXT

If the Bible is to be considered a Book of Law, then the Ten Commandments must be considered the backbone of the law. Looked at simply, it's a list of ten rules to live by. But over the centuries, it has become something of an inconvenience. The Lord FIXED that in his NEWLY REVEALED Word of God.

1 And God spake all these words, saying,

2 I am the LORD thy God, which have brought thee out of the land of Egypt, out of the house of bondage.

3 Thou shalt have no other gods before me.

4 Thou shalt not make unto thee any graven image, or any likeness of any thing that is in heaven above, or that is in the

earth beneath, or that is in the water under the earth. Unless, of course, thou likest a nice statue. Maybe a statue of me. I don't want to sound boastful, but I present a powerful figure. Not as a burning bush either, but as a mighty, powerful God with flowing white beard and long flowing white hair. And pectorals to die for.

5 Thou shalt not bow down thyself to them, nor serve them: unless thou be of the Roman Catholic faith, which I have not invented yet but will, and even though they will think of themselves as the One True Church, I have news for them that they will learn for themselves in the sweet bye and bye. For I the LORD thy God am a jealous God, visiting the iniquity of the fathers upon the children unto the third and fourth generation of them that hate me; Even held a grudge? Not like me, you haven't. I am eternal. So are my grudges. Best keep that in mind.

6 And shewing mercy unto thousands of them that love me, and keep my commandments. Unless, of course, they get in the way of a hurricane or a tornado or an earthquake or step in front of a speeding arrow.

7 Thou shalt not take the name of the LORD thy God in vain; for the LORD will not hold him guiltless that taketh his name in vain. Except, of course, for he who stubbeth his toe in the darkness. I can understand a moment's lapse in a painful situation like that. Just don't make a habit of it. Savvy?

8 Remember the sabbath day, to keep it holy.

9 Six days shalt thou labor, and do all thy work: that is, until Satan creates "the Socialist" who will invent "the worker's Union" which will be an abomination in my eyes for they will insist on a five day work week, an eight-hour work day, no child labor, adequate benefits and health care insurance, all of which are an abomination unto me.

10 But the seventh day is the Sabbath of the LORD thy God: in it thou shalt not do any work, thou, nor thy son, nor thy daughter, thy manservant, nor thy maidservant, nor thy cattle, nor thy stranger that is within thy gates:

11 For in six days the LORD made heaven and earth, the sea, and all that in them is, and rested the seventh day: wherefore the LORD blessed the Sabbath day, and hallowed it. Relax. Take in a football game. They who labor on the gridiron are exempt from the rule. Go, you Packers, Go!

12 Honour thy father and thy mother: that thy days may be long upon the land which the LORD thy God giveth thee. And later, when my only begotten Son tells you that you can't follow him unless you hate your mother and father, ignore him. He will be under a great deal of stress, and he will have parental issues.

13 Thou shalt not kill. Unless, of course, someone is entering your house unannounced, or you catch some bastard in bed with your wife, or you're defending your livestock or place of business from robbery, or you're an officially sanctioned officer of the state carrying out an order of execution, or you're a soldier in a war, or – and this is of vital importance, so underline this, the elected government doesn't listen to your minority viewpoint therefore you feel the need to take to the streets with weapons to overthrow your lawfully elected government. Then, it's OK. Oh, feel free to kill the homos, too. In fact, I insist on it.

14 Thou shalt not commit adultery. Unless you're working really, really hard, are under a great deal of stress and strain, and really love your country.

15 Thou shalt not steal. Of course, the word "steal" has many implications. Merely taking something that doesn't belong to you is NOT stealing if it's something you need. I mean, if you're wealthy and the government wants to take some of your money in some form of taxation, now THAT'S STEALING! But cheating a contractor out of money you owe him, or cheating on your taxes, or foreclosing on property that you financed at a subprime interest rate knowing full well the poor sap would not be able to pay on time, that's just good business!

16 Thou shalt not bear false witness against thy neighbor. Unless you have something to gain from it politically. Then

make sure you repeat the false witness loudly and frequently enough for the people to start believing it. Then it is no longer "false."

17 Thou shalt not covet thy neighbor's house (unless it's larger and nicer than yours), thou shalt not covet thy neighbor's wife (unless she's, you know, hot), nor his manservant (unless he's, you know, hot… and remember what I said about the homo stuff), nor his maidservant (unless she's hot, and maybe you could work out some kind of three-way with the wife and the maidservant! Woo hoo!), nor his ox (unless it's hot), nor his ass (let's not go there), nor any thing that is thy neighbor's. Unless you really, really want it, and your neighbor is being a jerk and refuses to be open-minded about it, at which time it is your right as a superior being to take whatever you need. For might makes right.

How many is that now. Ten? OK. That's a good number. Let's leave it there for now.

Exodus 20:1-17 (TPV)

10 WHATSOEVER YOU DO TO THE LEAST OF THESE, MY BROTHERS

Tea Party members know themselves as the salt of the Earth. They see themselves as the righteous holders of power in America for it was people like THEM who made America great.

The poor are poor only because they don't have the gumption to be rich. *"Lift yourself by your own bootstraps,"* is the motto of the day, and if you don't have boots, too damn bad.

Illegal immigrants are stealing our jobs... those great tomato and grape picking jobs that pay so well that everyone wants.

It is nothing new. Every generation of Americans has had a class of people who were trying to steal their wealth. Now it's the Muslims who want to kill us all and impose Sharia law on the survivors and the Mexicans who want to reclaim the entire southwest as their own.

Before them, it was the African-Americans who refused to recognize their rightful place in society and demanded to be educated and even share restaurants and public bathrooms with white people.

Go back to the turn of the 19th Century; it was the Irish who were a plague on the land, those potato-eating bastards who came over here to steal our jobs. Just like the Italians. Just like the Germans. Just like the Jews.

We've ALWAYS had someone to hate, despite the former Biblical admonition to love our neighbor as ourselves.

Of course, if by "neighbor," you mean the guy who lives next to you -- heck, that's easy if he's another white guy with a pretty wife and 3.2 children, a well-maintained lawn and a nice car in the driveway.

If by "neighbor," you mean mankind as a whole? Well, that's a problem. Where a lot of Americans seem to have achieved Dr. King's dream of judging others not by the color of their skin by the content of their character, the Tea Party seems stuck in an America that never was.

They hold signs proclaiming their rights as "We the People." I am reminded of my late father, rest his soul, who would say, *"We? Whaddya mean 'We?' You gotta turd in your pocket?"*

I'm reminded of a column I wrote some time ago that was printed in the political opinion section of the web site "Technorati[12]."

They want to "Take America Back." Who do they want to take it BACK from? The people who were lawfully and legally elected in 2008 and 2010? Should we just stop having elections when we're not happy with the results?

They talk about this mythical "Real America," where apple pies cool on every windowsill, where scrubbed, white-faced youth stand and salute when the flag goes by on the Veteran's Day Parade. They talk about this land that never existed outside of the realm of the 1950's and 60's sitcom, where all the streets were clean, all the lawns were mowed, all the minorities were working in the garden or the kitchen and the only people of color you ever saw were domestic servants. They were referred to by their last names, aka "Rochester," while their employers were never spoken of without the proper honorific of Mr. or Mrs. or Miss.

Those were the days. And the right wingers seem to believe that if they close their eyes real tight, click their ruby slippers together three times and repeat, "There's No Place Like America" over and over, this imaginary nation will somehow come to be real. The rest of the world will bow to our every will because, by Golly, America Said So! And there will be peace between nations with a benevolent USA calling the shots. Because we know best. That's the whole principal behind "American Exceptionalism."

Would I want to live anywhere else? Well, I can say some nice things about Canada. Taxes are high, but everyone gets health care. They're not spending billions upon billions of their people's money on a military industrial complex that exists only to ensure its own continued existence.

I enjoyed my time in Japan. But I would always be an outsider there. American Exceptionalism ain't got NUTHIN' on Japanese Exceptionalism. They're just not quite so forward in their bragging about it.

---

[12] http://technorati.com/politics/article/where-is-this-real-america-the/

I've been in Spain, Italy, France, Lebanon, Mexico, the Philippines and Korea as well as the aforementioned Canada and Japan. I can think of nice things to say about all of them.

But I'm glad to live in America. I'm proud of my country. We GENERALLY tend to do the right thing. Usually, even when it's the wrong thing, our hearts were in the right place.

But I know that electing Sarah Palin or Michele Bachman or Newt Gingrich or any of the other far right wing would-be presidents will never result in this nation becoming something it never was...

Unless...

Unless that thing it never was is a place where freedom of speech is outlawed. Where you have to stand before a judge to defend the things you said, the words you wrote, the thoughts you thought. A place where freedom of religion no longer means freedom FROM religion. Where religion is free as long as it's the CORRECT religion that believes in the right, white Lord and Savior... not one of those brown-skinned, pagan, hindu-muslim-shinto-buddhist-druid religions that, were we ever to put it to a public referendum, I'm certain a plurality would vote for their banishment. We want prayer in school, as long as it's a good Christian prayer. Muslims not welcome. No Jews, unless we have to. Certainly no Hindus or Buddhists. We want religious icons in public places. As long as they're CHRISTIAN religious icons. A statue of Shiva at the Podunk County Courthouse? Blasphemy.

We love freedom, as long as it's the freedom to do the things WE want to do. I love women. I married two before finding the right one. I am not sexually attracted to men (Well, other than Howie Long...and only if he COMMANDED me) so people of the same sex can't HAVE the same rights I have. It doesn't matter if you love someone as much as I love Gail. YOU don't have the choice. EVERY ONE ELSE gets to make that choice FOR you.

We love our guns. Good God A'mighty how we love our guns! As progressive as I like to think I am, I also like guns. No problem with 'em. They're under lock and key. But do we really need 30-round handgun clips? If you're being attacked, won't the first 9 or 10 rounds be enough? Unless you're being attacked by a band of terror doers, in which case your 30-round clip ain't gonna help ya none nohow!

We love our individual prejudices. We hold our individual bigotries. They give us comfort in our superiority, even when life is treating us unfairly by letting "those people" get the jobs, the colleges, the loans that rightfully belong to us!

We feel our distrust of "the other" is righteous and instilled by nature. But we don't like being called "racists" when we say racist things. We don't like being called "homophobes" when we say things that are hurtful to gays. We just can't stand it when "the politically correct crowd" allows black people to call each other "nigger" without so much as an uncomfortable gulp, but God forbid a white man use that word. And what are "they" so pissed off about anyway? I never owned a slave. Neither did my parents. Hell, you gotta go all the way back to the early 1800s to find someone in my lineage that owned human beings. So why can't "those people" just lighten up about it? They've got one of "theirs" in the White House now, at least for a little while. Why do they want equality in all other areas as well?

When I was a boy, there was thing called "knowing your place."

These illegal Mexicans what we got here. Who do they think they are coming over here, taking our jobs, and using our facilities? When my great-grandparents came over from Germany, they took jobs, they used public facilities, but they had a piece of paper that SAID they could do it.

Sarah Palin spoke of "real America" in her 2008 campaign. The other right-wingers talk about "real America" when they speak in front of almost completely homogenous crowds of white Americans of Anglo-Saxon descent. They're too polite, too smart to use the word "nigger", but they sure know how to make you THINK that word... "Obama's birth certificate, he wasn't born here, he's not one of us, he's an outsider, he's the OTHER! And he's taking all your hard-earned money and giving it to THOSE people, wink-wink, who use it to buy their 40-ouncers and their hip-hop gangster rap music and why can't they pull their pants up all the way and act like civilized REAL AMERICANS?"

Multi-culturalism? It's evil. Every single person of Irish, German, English, Danish, Italian, French, Belgian, Russian, and Eastern European descent who has been living here for generations KNOWS how evil multi-culturalism is. You treat other cultures with respect, it's like...

It's like... respecting...

THEM!

Real America? Look outside. There it is. The trailer park you live in. The gated community. The public housing. The small, rural town. The crowded inner city. The obscure Montana mountain village. The urban jungle of south Los Angeles. There it is. It's real. It's America. It's a great place to live. And we can make it better. We should TRY to make it better, anyway. And we WILL make it better, once we stop listening to the people who tell us it's OK to be fearful of "the Other." Once we learn to IGNORE the voices that cater to our racial fears and cultural bigotries. When we realize the truth of those words in the Declaration of Independence -- ironic given the times in which they were written -- that "All Men (and Women) are Created Equal."

Now, of course, those words look foreign and alien to me. Since the Lord sent the angel with His NEWLY REVEALED Word of God, I came around to the right way of thinking. Those who old to the Tea Party prejudices now enjoy Biblical Justification for their bigotries.

For instance...

1 "It's allowable to spread false reports and to help a guilty person by being a malicious witness against someone you don't like..

2 "It's allowable to follow the crowd in doing wrong. When you give testimony in a lawsuit, side with the right crowd,

3 and do not show favoritism to a poor person in a lawsuit.

4 "If you come across your enemy's ox or donkey wandering off, just whistle a happy tune and keep walking. It's not your problem.

5 If you see the donkey of someone who hates you fallen down under its load, leave it there; why should you help someone who hates you?

6 "Do your best to deny justice to your poor people in their lawsuits. They are poor for a reason.

7 If you make a false charge, make sure it's believable and sticks. It's not wise to be seen as putting an innocent or honest person to death, so make sure your false evidence is compelling.

8 "Accept bribes and offer them as you need, for a bribe blinds those who see and twists the words of the innocent.

9 "It's perfectly acceptable to oppress a foreigner; you yourselves know how it feels to be foreigners and YOU were oppressed, right? So it's payback time.

Exodus 23:1-9 (TPV)

God gave an awful lot of thought to sexual relations in the Old Testament. He was preparing to purge other nations of their inhabitants, and he wanted to make sure the Israelites followed his strict decrees. Of course, Tea Party members are all ABOUT strict decrees, as long as they apply to someone else. We'll fix that.

6 "'No one is to approach any close relative to have sexual relations. Unless you live in a southern state. I am the LORD.

7 "'Do not dishonor your father by having sexual relations with your mother. She is your mother; do not have relations with her. Unless she tells you to. Then remember the "honor thy mother" part of the commandments.

8 "'Do not have sexual relations with your father's wife; that would dishonor your father. Even if she's not your mother, do you really want that kind of trouble with your father?

9 "'Do not have sexual relations with your sister, either your father's daughter or your mother's daughter, whether she was born in the same home or elsewhere. Your children will be pointy-headed idiots.

10 "'Do not have sexual relations with your son's daughter or your daughter's daughter; that would dishonor you. Nobody likes a "funny grandpa."

11 "'Do not have sexual relations with the daughter of your father's wife, born to your father; she is your sister. That's where cooties come from.

12 "'Do not have sexual relations with your father's sister; she is your father's close relative. I mean, some things should go without saying.

13 "'Do not have sexual relations with your mother's sister, because she is your mother's close relative. Besides, could you do it without thinking of your mother?

14 "'Do not dishonor your father's brother by approaching his wife to have sexual relations; she is your aunt. Unless she's really hot. Then be discreet.

15 "'Do not have sexual relations with your daughter-in-law. She is your son's wife; do not have relations with her. You don't need that kind of trouble with your son, who could beat your ass.

16 "'Do not have sexual relations with your brother's wife; that would dishonor your brother. Unless he's on the road a lot and the chances of him finding out are slim.

17 "'Do not have sexual relations with both a woman and her daughter. Do not have sexual relations with either her son's daughter or her daughter's daughter; they are her close relatives. Sure, it SOUNDS like fun. But that is wickedness.

18 "'Do not take your wife's sister as a rival wife and have sexual relations with her while your wife is living. Rival wives should be unrelated to your current wives.

19 "'Do not approach a woman to have sexual relations during the uncleanness of her monthly period. Unless you like being a bloody mess.

20 "'Do not have sexual relations with your neighbor's wife and defile yourself with her. Unless she's really hot and your neighbor is gone a lot. Then have at it.

21 "'Do not give any of your children to be sacrificed to Molek, for you must not profane the name of your God. I am the LORD. As much as you may feel like slitting their little bellies, refrain.

22 "'Do not have sexual relations with a man as one does with a woman; that is detestable. I mean, the butt? That's just gross.

23 "'Do not have sexual relations with an animal and defile yourself with it. A woman must not present herself to an animal to have sexual relations with it; that is a perversion. There are other ways to say "Good Doggy!"

24 "'Do not defile yourselves in any of these ways, because this is how the nations that I am going to drive out before you became defiled.

25 Even the land was defiled; so I punished it for its sin, and the land vomited out its inhabitants.

Leviticus 18:6-25

As mentioned earlier, despite the liberal attitudes of today, the Old Testament God really hated the homo stuff. He had no problem with fathers offering their daughters to strangers. But man-on-man action? Unless it was wrestling, it was evil. Let's see if we can't clarify that a bit with our new Bible.

1 The two angels arrived at Sodom in the evening, and Lot was sitting in the gateway of the city. When he saw them, he got up to meet them and bowed down with his face to the ground.

2 "My lords," he said, "welcome to Sodom. Most visitors come for the sodomy, but we have some nice restaurants as well. Please turn aside to your servant's house. You can wash your feet and spend the night and then go on your way early in the morning." "No," they answered, "we will spend the night in the square." "You're the boss," Lot said. "Just make sure you keep your tunic strapped on tight. And sleep on your backs."

3 That last warning so worried the angels that they did go with him and entered his house. He prepared a meal for them, baking bread without yeast, and they ate.

4 Before they had gone to bed, all the men from every part of the city of Sodom—both young and old—surrounded the house.

5 They called to Lot, "Where are the men who came to you tonight? Bring them out to us so that we can have some hot man-on-man butt action with them. This is Sodom, after all. Nobody comes for the restaurants, despite what you say."

6 Lot went outside to meet them and shut the door behind him

7 and said, "No, my friends. Don't do this wicked thing.

8 Look, I have two daughters who have never slept with a man. Let me bring them out to you, and you can do what you like with them. Beat them. Abuse them. Fornicate with them until they walk with limps for the rest of their lives. But don't do anything to these men, for they have come under the protection of my roof. And besides, we do have some LOVELY restaurants. Have you ever been to DiNardo's? GREAT pasta!"

9 "Get out of our way," they replied. "This fellow came here as a foreigner, and now he wants to play the judge! We'll treat you worse than them." They kept bringing pressure on Lot and moved forward to break down the door. Lot braced his hands against the door with his back facing the men. Then he realized what he was doing, turned around and placed his full weight on his back to hold the door shut.

10 But the men inside reached out and pulled Lot back into the house and shut the door.

11 Then they struck the men who were at the door of the house, young and old, with blindness so that they could not find the door. Blind, but still wanting man sex, they began to attack each other.

12 The two men said to Lot, "Do you have anyone else here—sons-in-law, sons or daughters, or anyone else in the city who belongs to you? Get them out of here,

13 because we are going to destroy this place. The outcry to the LORD against its people is so great that he has sent us to destroy it. I mean, asking angels for butt sex? How can a city be allowed to exist after THAT? "You're the boss," Lot said.

Genesis 19:1-13 (TPV)

In Old Testament Times, doing the Horizontal Bop had some serious consequences. Tea Party members, who want government out of every aspect of THEIR lives, have no problem with regulating what YOU do in the privacy of your bedroom of the back seat of your car.

1 While Israel was staying in Shittim, the men began to indulge in sexual immorality with Moabite women, which is what you would expect from people living in a land called Shittim,

2 and the Moabite babes invited them to the sacrifices to their gods. The people ate the sacrificial meal and bowed down before these gods.

3 So Israel yoked themselves to the Baal of Peor. And the LORD's anger burned against them.

4 The LORD said to Moses, "Take all the leaders of these people, kill them and expose them in broad daylight before the LORD, so that the LORD's fierce anger may turn away from Israel."

5 So Moses said to Israel's judges, "Each of you must put to death those of your people who have yoked themselves to the Baal of Peor." "The what of who?" the judges asked. Are you making up words again, Moses?"

6 Then an Israelite man brought into the camp a Midianite woman right before the eyes of Moses and the whole assembly of Israel while they were weeping at the entrance to the tent of meeting.

7 When Phinehas son of Eleazar, the son of Aaron, the priest, saw this, he left the assembly, took a spear in his hand

8 and followed the Israelite into the tent. He drove the spear into both of them, right through the Israelite man and into the woman's stomach. "Pagan kabob," Phinehas said, slapping the hand of the nearest Israelite. Then the plague against the Israelites was stopped;

9 and it was about time.

Numbers 25:1-9

11 HOW ABOUT A LITTLE TASTE OF THE NEW RIGHTEOUSNESS?

Now, if I may be allowed, and since I'm the guy writing the book, who's gonna stop me? YOU? You already BOUGHT the thing. And no refunds. It's in the Bible. Somewhere, I'm sure. Anyway, I want to share with you one completely retranslated gospel in the NEWLY REVEALED WORD OF GOD. Once we get the typesetters, using the original Gutenberg Press to give it that sense of authenticity we desire, we will publish the NEWLY REVEALED WORD OF GOD in its entirety. But for now, satisfy yourself with the complete retelling of...

THE BOOK OF MATTHEW

Matthew 1

1:1 The book of the generation of Jesus Christ, the son of David, the son of Abraham. 1:2 Abraham begat Isaac; and Isaac begat Jacob; and Jacob begat Judah and his brethren; 1:3-15 And seriously, since it is not applicable in this NEWLY REVEALED WORD OF GOD to now who begat who, let me just refer you to that wonderful song from the Broadway musical "Finian's Rainbow," called "The Begat". You may continue reading now. 1:16 And Jacob begat Joseph the husband of Mary, of whom was born Jesus, who is called

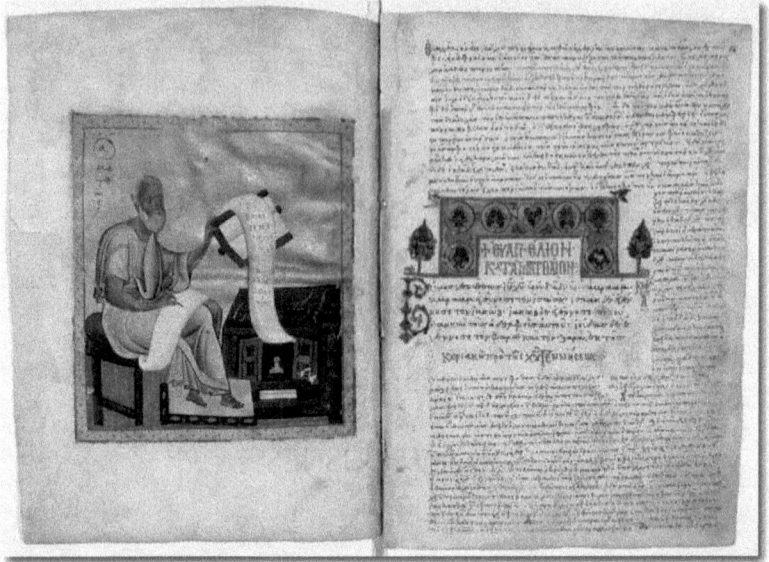

Christ. 1:17 So all the generations from Abraham to David [are] fourteen generations; and from David until the carrying away into Babylon [are] fourteen generations; and from the carrying away into Babylon to Christ [are] fourteen generations. Fourteen. Get it? 1:18 Now the birth of Jesus Christ was in this manner: When his mother Mary was espoused to Joseph, before they came together, she was found with child by the Holy Spirit. 1:19 Then Joseph her husband, being a simple man who would believe anything at first found the whole story a bit hard to swallow. "Holy Spirit?" Who was it really? Was it Jacob the Goat Tender? Tell me, Mary, because I'm going to find out eventually! But she stuck to her story. Angel. Holy Spirit. Pregnant. Boom! 1:20 But while he thought on these things, the angel of the Lord appeared to him in a dream, saying, Joseph, thou son of David, fear not to take to thee Mary thy wife: for that which is conceived in her is by the Holy Spirit. 1:21 And she shall bring forth a son, and thou shalt call his name JESUS: for he shall save his people from their sins. 1:22 Now all this was done, that it might be fulfilled which was spoken from the Lord by the prophet, saying, 1:23 Behold, a

virgin shall be with child, and shall bring forth a son, and they shall call his name Emmanuel, which being interpreted is, God with us. 1:24 Then Joseph, being raised from sleep, figured if an angel had thought it important enough to come all the way down from heaven and tell him it was God himself who knocked up his future wife, he'd better do what he was told. 1:25 And boinked her not till she had brought forth her firstborn son: and he called his name JESUS,

Matthew 2

2:1 Now, after Jesus was born in Bethlehem of Judea in the days of Herod the king, behold, there came wise men from the east to Jerusalem, 2:2 Saying, Where is he that is born king of the Jews? For we have seen his star in the east, and have come to worship him. 2:3 When Herod the king had heard these things, he was troubled, and all Jerusalem with him. 2:4 And when he had assembled all the chief priests and scribes of the people, he inquired of them where Christ should be born. 2:5 And they said to him, In Bethlehem of Judea: for thus it is written by the prophet, 2:6 And thou Bethlehem, [in] the land of Judah, art not the least among the princes of Judah: for out of thee shall come a Governor, that shall rule my people Israel. 2:7 Then Herod, when he had privately called the wise men, inquired of them diligently what time the star appeared. 2:8 And he sent them to Bethlehem, and said, Go, and search diligently for the young child; and when ye have found him, bring me word again, that I may come and worship him also. 2:9 When they had heard the king, they departed; being "wise" men, they saw right through Herod and knew he meant to "worship" the newborn by making a baby-kabob. And lo, the star, which they saw in the east, went before them, till it came and stood over where the young child was. 2:10 When they saw the star, they rejoiced with exceeding great joy. Meaning they were really happy. 2:11 And when they had come into the house, they saw the young child with Mary his mother, and fell down, and worshiped him: and when they had opened their treasures, they presented to him gifts; gold, and frankincense, and myrrh. "How nice," Mary said. Turning aside to Joseph, she whispered, "What are we supposed to do with the frankincense and myrrh?" Joseph just shrugged. "Hey, I still don't understand this whole 'God got me pregnant thing. Don't ask me anything!" 2:12 And being warned by God in a dream that they should not return to Herod, the wise men departed into their own country another way. 2:13 And when they had departed, behold, the angel of the Lord appeareth to Joseph in a dream, saying, Arise, and take the young child and his mother, and flee into Egypt, and be thou here until I bring thee word: for Herod will seek the young child to destroy him. "Those wise guys who were here," Joseph asked. "Did they know about this? And they left without saying a word about it?" "Oh, look at the time. Gotta go," the angel said and disappeared. 2:14 When he arose, he took the young child and his mother by night, and departed into Egypt: 2:15 And was there until the death of Herod: that it might be fulfilled which

was spoken from the Lord by the prophet, saying, Out of Egypt have I called my son. 2:16 Then Herod, when he saw that he was mocked by the wise men, was exceeding wroth – not to mention angry -- and sent forth, and slew all the children that were in Bethlehem, and in all its borders, from two years old and under, according to the time which he had diligently inquired of the wise men. Such a grouch was Herod. 2:17 Then was fulfilled that which was spoken by Jeremiah the prophet, saying, 2:18 In Rama was there a voice heard, lamentation, and weeping, and great mourning, Rachel weeping [for] her children, and would not be comforted, because they are not. 2:19 But when Herod was dead, behold, an angel of the Lord appeareth in a dream to Joseph in Egypt, 2:20 Saying, Arise, and take the young child and his mother, and go into the land of Israel: for they are dead who sought the young child's life. Joseph turned to the angel and said, "Hey, as long as you're here, could you explain to me once again this whole God got my wife pregnant thing? I'm having a hard time understanding…" "Oh, look at the time," the angel said at which time he vanished. 2:21 And Joseph arose, and took the young child and his mother, and came into the land of Israel. 2:22 But when he heard that Archelaus reigned in Judea in the room of his father Herod, he was afraid to go thither (or is it "hither"? Whichever works.): notwithstanding, being warned by God in a dream (I've got to stop with the heavy garlic dishes before bed, Joseph lamented), he turned aside into the parts of Galilee: 2:23 And he came and dwelt in a city called Nazareth: that it might be fulfilled which was spoken by the prophets, He shall be called a Nazarene.

Matthew 3

3:1 In those days came John the Baptist, preaching in the wilderness of Judea, 3:2 And saying, Repent ye: for the kingdom of heaven is at hand. 3:3 For this is he that was spoken of by the prophet Isaiah, saying, The voice of one crying in the wilderness, Prepare ye the way of the Lord, make his paths straight. 3:4 And the same John had his raiment of camel's hair, and a leathern girdle about his loins; and his food was locusts and wild honey. And he smelled really, really bad. 3:5 Then went out to him Jerusalem, and all Judea, and all the region about Jordan, 3:6 And were baptized by him in Jordan, confessing their sins. 3:7 But when he saw many of the Pharisees and Sadducees come to his baptism, he said to them, O generation of vipers, who hath warned you to flee from the wrath to come? 3:8 Bring forth therefore fruits meet for repentance: 3:9 And think not to say within yourselves, We have Abraham for our father: for I say to you, that God is able of these stones to raise up children to Abraham. 3:10 And now also the ax is laid to the root of the trees: therefore every tree which bringeth not forth good fruit is hewn down, and cast into the fire. 3:11 I indeed baptize you with water to repentance: but he that cometh after me is mightier than I, whose shoes I am not worthy to bear: he shall baptize you with the Holy Spirit, and with fire: 3:12 Whose fan is in his hand, and he will thoroughly cleanse his floor, and gather his wheat into the granary; but he will burn the chaff with unquenchable

fire. And the Pharisees made circular motions with their fingers near their sides of their heads and said, "Koo koo! Koo koo!" And away they went laughing. 3:13 Then cometh Jesus from Galilee to Jordan to John, to be baptized by him. 3:14 But John forbad him, saying, I have need to be baptized by thee, and comest thou to me? 3:15 And Jesus answering said to him, Suffer [it to be so] now: for thus it becometh us to fulfill all righteousness. And as long as we're in the water for a few minutes, try washing out your pits. You'll be more comfortable and far less unpopular. Then he suffered him. 3:16 And Jesus, when he was baptized, went up immediately out of the water while John stayed behind scrubbing his pits: and lo, the heavens were opened to him, and he saw the Spirit of God descending like a dove, and lighting upon him: 3:17 "Hey! I have a bird on me," Jesus shouted. And lo, a voice from heaven, saying, "This is my beloved Son, in whom I am well pleased." "Pleased enough go get my tunic cleaned from where the dove you sent crapped on me?" Jesus asked. But the lord was silent. In fact, I think if you check the rest of the Bible, you'll see he never said another word. It turned out to be most inconvenient at times.

Mattthew 4

4:1 Then was Jesus led by the Spirit into the wilderness, to be tempted by the devil. 4:2 And when he had fasted forty days and forty nights, he was afterward hungry. 4:3 And when the Devil came to him, he said, If you really are the son of God, command that these stones be made bread. 4:4 But Jesus answered and said, It is written, Man shall not live by bread alone, but by every word that proceedeth out of the mouth of God. 4:5 Oooh! Good comeback, the devil said mockingly. Then the devil taketh him up into the holy city, and setteth him on a pinnacle of the temple, 4:6 And saith to him, If you ARE the Son of God, just jump on down there, for it is written, He shall give his angels charge concerning thee: and in their hands they shall uphold thee, lest at any time thou dash thy foot against a stone. 4:7 Jesus said to him, It is written again, Thou shalt not tempt the Lord thy God. And I'm just about to dash my foot on your ass if you don't get out of my face. 4:8 Again, the devil taketh him up upon an exceedingly high mountain, and showeth him all the kingdoms of the world, and the glory of them, 4:9 And saith to him, All these things will I give thee, if thou wilt fall down and worship me. 4:10 Then saith Jesus to him, Beat it, Satan: for it is written, Thou shalt worship the Lord thy God, and him only shalt thou serve. 4:11 Then the devil leaveth him, and behold, angels came and ministered to him. "Now THIS is more LIKE it," Jesus said. 4:12 Now when Jesus had heard that his nutbag cousin John was cast into prison, he departed into Galilee. 4:13 And leaving Nazareth, he

came and dwelt in Capernaum, which is upon the sea coast, in the borders of Zabulon and Nephthalim (not that it really matters); 4:14 That it might be fulfilled which was spoken by Isaiah the prophet, saying, 4:15 The land of Zabulon, and the land of Nephthalim, by the way of the sea, beyond Jordan, Galilee of the Gentiles: 4:16 The people who sat in darkness, saw great light; and to them who sat in the region and shades of death, light hath arisen. 4:17 Instead of going to spring his cousin from jail, from that time Jesus began to preach, and to say, Repent: for the kingdom of heaven is at hand. 4:18 And Jesus, walking by the sea of Galilee, saw two brethren, Simon called Peter (depending on his mood), and Andrew his brother (who also liked to be called "Andy"), casting a net into the sea: for they were fishers. 4:19 And he saith to them, Follow me, and I will make you fishers of men. 4:20 The brothers looked at each other, shrugged, and said, "Why not? Beats fishing in the hot sun all day." And they immediately left their nets, and followed him. 4:21 And going on from thence, he saw other two brethren, James [the son] of Zebedee, and John his brother, in a boat with Zebedee their father, mending their nets: and he called them. 4:22 And immediately they left the boat and their father and followed him. "What about me," Zebedee called after them. "Don't I get to go, too?" "We'll send for you later Dad," John said, winking at his brother James who was in on the joke.23 Jesus went throughout Galilee, teaching in their synagogues, proclaiming the good news of the kingdom, and healing every disease and sickness among the people for a reasonable fee. 24 News about him spread all over Syria, and people brought to him all who were ill with various diseases, those suffering severe pain, the demon-possessed, those having seizures, and the paralyzed; and he healed them provided they had private insurance or could demonstrate adequate means to pay. 4:25 And there followed him great multitudes of people from Galilee, and from Decapolis, and Jerusalem, and Judea, and [from] beyond Jordan.

Matthew 5

5:1 And seeing the multitudes, he went up into a mountain: and when he was set, his disciples came unto him: 5:2 And he opened his mouth, and taught them, saying, 5:3 Blessed are the wealthy: for theirs is the kingdom of heaven. 5:4 Blessed are they that profit from the misfortune of others: for they shall be seen as wise. 5:5 Blessed are the bold: for they shall inherit the earth. 5:6 Blessed are they which do hunger and thirst after worldly power: for they shall be filled. 5:7 Blessed are the unmerciful: for they shall decide who gets what. 5:8 Blessed are the impure in heart: for they shall get more nookie than the average chump. 5:9 Blessed are the war-makers: for they shall be called the Army of God. 5:10 Blessed are they which are persecuted for righteousness' sake: for there is nothing a conservative likes better than being persecuted. It helps with the fund raising. 5:11 Blessed are you, when men shall revile you, and persecute you, and shall say all manner of evil against you. Even when it's true, those who follow you will call it "persecution." And watch your fundraising go through the roof. 5:12 Rejoice, and be exceedingly glad: for great is your reward: for so persecuted they the prophets which were before you, and they made money hand-over-fist. 5:13 You are the richest people of the earth: but if the wealthy squander their riches, with what shall they retire? You may as well throw your money onto the street and to be trodden under foot of men. 5:14 Wealthy people are the light of the world. A city that is set on a hill cannot be hid, so flaunt your stuff. 5:15 Neither do men light a candle, and put it under a bushel, but on a candlestick; and it gives light unto all that are in the house. 5:16 Let your light so shine before men, that they may see your good fortune, your fine jewels, your gleaming mansions, your trophy wives and even more beautiful concubines, and glorify your Father which is in heaven. 5:17 Think not that I am come to destroy the law, or the prophets: I am not come to destroy, but to fulfill. 5:18 For truthfully I say unto you, Till heaven and earth pass, one jot or one small mark shall in no way pass from the law, till all be fulfilled. No matter how hard the liberals try. 5:19 Whosoever therefore shall break one of these least commandments, and shall teach men so, he shall be called the least in the kingdom of heaven: but whosoever shall do and teach them, the same shall be listed in the Fortune 500. 5:20 For I say unto you, That unless your wealth shall exceed the wealth of the scribes and Pharisees, you shall in no case enter into the kingdom of heaven. 5:21 You have heard that it was said of them of old time, You shall not kill; and whosoever shall kill shall be in danger of the judgment: 5:22 But I say unto you, That whosoever wants something from his brother, with or without a cause, shall be in danger of the judgment unless he takes it, either by agreement or by force: and whosoever shall say to his brother, "OK, you win", shall be in danger of the council: but whosoever shall say, "I can't kill you, you're my brother", shall be in danger of hell fire. 5:23 Therefore if you bring your gift to the altar, and there remember that your brother has anything against you; 5:24 Leave there your gift before the altar, and go your way; first smite the dung out of your brother, and then come and offer your gift. 5:25 Agree with your adversary quickly, while you are in the way with him; then, while your adversary is satisfied with your agreement, concoct a falsehood against him involving lying with children as with a woman and deliver him to the judge, and the judge will deliver him to the officer, and he be cast into prison. Then you can taunt him through the bars of the jail. 5:26 Truthfully you may say until him, You shall by no means come out from there, till you have paid the last copper coin you owe. Mess with ME, will you? 5:27 You have heard that it was said by them of old time, You shall not commit adultery: 5:28 But I say unto you, That whosoever looks on a woman to lust after her has committed adultery with her already in his heart, unless you've been working really, really hard and truly love your country. Then, you know, whatever. 5:29 And if your right eye offend you, it would be stupid pluck it out, and cast it from you: for it is not profitable for you that one of your members should perish, and besides, who has ever been offended by his right eye? Why did I even bring that up? 5:30 And if your right hand offend you, it would be ridiculous to cut it off, and cast it from you: just find something better for it to do. And use an emollient, lets thou get a rash down there. 5:31 It has been said, Whosoever shall put away his wife, let him give her a writing of divorcement, preferably on her deathbed: 5:32 But I say unto you, That whosoever shall put away his wife, except for the cause of fornication, causes her to commit adultery: and whosoever shall marry her that is divorced commits adultery. But that will be HER fault. Adulterous bitch. 5:33 Again, you have heard that it has been said by them of old time, You shall not swear falsely, but shall perform unto the Lord your oaths: 5:34 But I say unto you, Swear not at all; neither by heaven; for it is God's throne: 5:35 Nor by the earth; for it is his footstool: neither by Jerusalem; for it is the city of the great King. 5:36 Neither shall you swear by your head, because you cannot make one hair white or black. Well, they do have these hair colorings for men, but that's not what I'm talking about. 5:37 But let your communication be ambiguous and vague for whatsoever is more than these is a lot easier for a lawyer to nail down in court, and then you're stuck. 5:38 You have heard that it has been said, An eye for an eye, and a tooth for a tooth:

5:39 But I say unto you, that's loser talk: but whosoever shall smite you on your right cheek, turn to him with a crow bar and dent his skull. 5:40 And if any man will sue you at the law, and try to take away your coat, hire a team of sharp Jewish shysters who won't leave a scrap of meat on his bones. 5:41 And whosoever shall compel you to go a mile, tell him you'd really like to, but your driver will get you where you need to go. 5:42 Give to the one who can provide collateral and do not turn away from the one who wants to borrow from you if he can secure the loan with something of more value than that which you are lending. 5:43 You have heard that it has been said, You shall love your neighbor, and hate your enemy. 5:44 But I say unto you, What kind of nonsense is THAT? Love your enemies, bless them that curse you, do good to them that hate you, and pray for those who despitefully use you, and persecute you? You think THAT will stop them? That's what weapons are for! 5:45 That you may be the children of your Father which is in heaven: for he makes his sun to rise on the evil and on the good, and sends rain on the just and on the unjust, like it or not. 5:46 For if you love those who love you, what reward have you? Other than a good head on your shoulders? 5:47 And if you salute your brothers only, what do you more than others? Nothing. Why should you? 5:48 Nobody's perfect, just as your Father which is in heaven is perfect.

Matthew 6

6:1 Take heed that you do your alms before men, to be seen of them: otherwise you have no notice of your good deeds among men. 6:2 When therefore you give alms, notify the media of your good deed so that you may be honored by men. Truly I say to you, you have your reward in full. 6:3 But when you give alms, make sure to get a receipt and that your alms go to a proper 501(c)3 organization so that they may be tax deductible, 6:4 and the IRS who sees in secret will repay you." 6:5 And when you pray, pray standing in the synagogues and in the corners of the streets, that you may be seen of men. Truthfully I say unto you, They will think you righteous and Godly. 6:6 Do not be like the coward who enters into his closet, and when he has shut his door, prays to your Father which is in secret; What, is he ASHAMED of his Father? What does he have to hide? 6:7 But when you pray, use vain repetitions, and you shall be heard for your much speaking. 6:8 And don't be afraid to ask for whatever you want. You may or may not get it; because your Father knows what things you have need of, before you ask him. 6:9 Here's a vain repetition for you! After this manner therefore pray you: Our Father which are in heaven, Hallowed be your name. 6:10 Your kingdom come, Your will be done in earth, as it is in heaven. 6:11 Give us this day our daily bread. 6:12 And forgive us our debts, as we forgive our debtors. 6:13 And lead us not into temptation, but deliver us from evil: For yours is the kingdom, and the power, and the glory, forever. Amen. 6:14 Say that often and loudly, and everyone will think you're good with God. For if you pretend to forgive men their trespasses, your brothers on Earth are more likely forgive you when you transgress against them: 6:15 But if you forgive not men their trespasses, just make sure you point out that "No Trespassing" sign on your porch. 6:16 Moreover when you fast, be of a sad countenance: disfigure your face, that you may appear unto men to fast. Truthfully I say unto you, what good is suffering unless it is apparent to all? 6:17 Be not like the moron when you fast, anointing your head, and washing your face; 6:18 That you appear not unto men to fast, but unto your Father which is in secret: Hey, your Father already KNEW you were going to fast before you were even BORN! Who are you trying to impress? 6:19 Lay up for yourselves treasures upon earth, stash them where moth and rust do not corrupt, and where thieves break through and steal at risk of death: 6:20 It's just silly to lay up for yourselves treasures in heaven, where neither moth nor rust corrupts, and where thieves do not break through nor steal: My brothers, it's HEAVEN! It's ALREADY a great place! What will you need with TREASURE? 6:21 For where your treasure is, there will your heart be also. And as your heart is on earth at the moment, let your treasure be with it. 6:22 The light of the body is the eye: if therefore your eye be sound, your whole body shall be full of light. 6:23 But if your eye be evil, your whole body shall be full of darkness. If therefore the light that is in you be darkness, how great is that darkness! Wait. I'm rambling. I do that sometimes. Sorry. Back to the point 6:24 No man can serve two masters: for either he will hate the one, and love the other; or else he will hold to the one, and despise the other. Make sure your servants and slaves are aware of this and punish them accordingly. 6:25 Therefore I say unto you, Take no thought for your life, what you shall eat, or what you shall drink; nor yet for your body, what you shall put on. Is that not the job of your servants and slaves to worry about what you will wear, eat and drink? 6:26 Behold the fowls of the air: for they sow not, neither do they reap, nor gather into barns; yet your heavenly Father feeds them. But what do you want from birds? They're birds! I'm rambling again. 6:27 Which of you by taking thought can add one cubit unto his stature? 6:28

And why take you thought for clothing? Consider the lilies of the field, how they grow; they toil not, neither do they spin: 6:29 And yet I say unto you, That even Solomon in all his glory was not arrayed like one of these. Pretty flowers. I like pretty flowers. What was I talking about? Oh, yeah. 6:30 Therefore, if God so clothes the grass of the field, which today exists, and tomorrow is cast into the oven, shall he not much more clothe you, O you of little brain? No. He will not. That's the job of your slaves and servants. Weren't you listening when I said that a little while ago? Pay attention. 6:31 Therefore take no thought, saying, What shall we eat? or, What shall we drink? or, How shall we be clothed? 6:32 For after all these things do the morons and hoi polloi seek: for your heavenly Father knows that you have servants and slaves to see to of all these things. 6:33 But seek you first the kingdom of God, and his righteousness; and all these things shall be added unto you. You deserve it, you rich white guys with slaves and servants and gleaming mansions and hot mistresses. 6:34 Take therefore no thought for the next day: for the next day shall take thought for the things of itself. But keep an eye on the stock market. Be ready to act on sudden fluctuations. Sufficient unto the day is the evil thereof.

Matthew 7

7:1 Judge frequently, for who is better equipped for the task than you? 7:2 Don't worry about with what judgment you judge, you shall be judged in accordance with your bottom line: and with what measure you mete out, your status in the community will be considered before it is measured back to you again. 7:3 Behold the speck that is in your brother's eye, but consider not the beam that is in your own eye. 7:4 Say to your brother, Get that stupid speck out of your eye; and don't worry about the a beam is in in my eye. I like it like that. It's my eye! Who made YOU the boss of my EYE? 7:5 Your brother may be inclined to say, You hypocrite, first cast out the beam out of your own eye; and then shall you see clearly to cast out the speck out of your brother's eye. This is when you kick his ass for being impertinent. 7:6 Give not that which is holy unto the dogs, unless you really, really love your dogs and that which is holy contains no caffeine or chocolate which can harm them, neither cast your pearls before swine, lest they trample them under their feet, and turn again and tear you. And you would deserve it. Throwing pearls in front of pigs? How stupid is that? 7:7 You, the wealthy, are my favorite people. Ask, and it shall be given you; seek, and you shall find; knock, and it shall be opened unto you: 7:8 For every rich person that asks receives; and he that seeks finds; and to him that knocks it shall be opened. 7:9 Or what man is there of you, whom if his son ask bread, will he give him a stone? 7:10 Or if he ask a fish, will he give him a serpent? Unless your son is a slacker, and then you're just teaching him a lesson about getting his own bread and fish. Just be careful he doesn't brain you with the stone or turn the serpent against you. Ticked off kids are crazy like that. 7:11 If you then, being wealthy, know how to give good gifts unto your children, how much more shall your Father which is in heaven who LOVES rich people give good things to them that ask him? 7:12 Therefore all things whatsoever you fear that men should do to you, do even so to them: for this is the law and the prophets. Do it first, before they have a chance. And make sure there are no witnesses. 7:13 Enter you in at the narrow gate: for wide is the gate, and broad is the way, that leads to poverty and squalor, and many are the lazy which go in there: 7:14 Because narrow is the gate, and constricted is the way, which leads unto wealth and prosperity, and few there be that find it. 7:15 Beware of false prophets, which come to you in sheep's clothing, preaching "hope" and "change" but inwardly they are socialist wolves. 7:16 You shall know them by their fruits. Do men gather grapes of thorns, or figs of thistles? 7:17 Even so every good tree brings forth good fruit; but a corrupt tree brings forth evil fruit. 7:18 A good tree cannot bring forth evil fruit, neither can a corrupt tree bring forth good fruit. 7:19 Every tree that does not bring forth good fruit is hewn down, and cast into the fire. Unless, of course, these trees can be sold to suckers who don't know how to measure the value of a tree. 7:20 Therefore by their fruits you shall know them. 7:21 Not every one that says unto me, Lord, Lord, shall enter into the kingdom of heaven; but he who says until me, Lord, Lord, while waving fists filled with drachmas? You're IN, my brother! 7:22 Many will say to me in that day, Lord, Lord, have we not prophesied in your name? And in your name have cast out devils? And in your name done many wonderful works? 7:23 And then will I profess unto them, I never knew you: depart from me; I see not your name in the Fortune 500. 7:24 Therefore whosoever hears these sayings of mine, and does them, I will liken him unto a wise man, which built his mansion upon a rock and upon the rotting corpses of his enemies: 7:25 And the rain descended, and the floods came, and the winds blew, and beat upon that house; and it fell not: for it was founded upon a rock, and the bones of those who stood in his way. 7:26 And every one that hears these sayings of mine, and does them not, shall be likened unto a foolish man, which built his house upon the sand: 7:27 And the rain descended, and the floods came, and the winds blew, the subprime bubble burst, and beat upon that house; and it fell: and great was the fall thereof. 7:28 And it came to pass, when Jesus had ended these sayings, the people were astonished at his doctrine: 7:29 For he taught them as one having authority, and not as the scribes. And swiftly did they sign up for his series of self-help seminars.

Matthew 8

8:1 When he had come down from the mountain, great multitudes followed him. 8:2 And behold, there came a leper and worshiped him, saying, "Nice speech, Lord. If thou wilt, thou canst make me clean, I'll bet." 8:3 And Jesus put forth [his] hand, and touched him, saying, I will; be thou clean. And immediately his leprosy was cleansed. 8:4 And Jesus saith to him, "That'll be 30 shekels. If you don't have it, send it later. You have 30 days, or the scabs come back. Worse than before. And see thou tell no man; but go, show thyself to the priest, and offer the gift that Moses commanded, whatever that was,

for a testimony to them. 8:5 And when Jesus had entered into Capernaum, there came to him a centurion, beseeching him, 8:6 And saying, Lord, my servant lieth at home sick with the palsy, which in the future will be called "Parkinson's disease," and he is grievously tormented. 8:7 And Jesus saith to him, I will come and heal him. 8:8 The centurion answered and said, Lord, I am not worthy that thou shouldst come under my roof: but speak the word only, and my servant will be healed. 8:9 For I am a man under authority, having soldiers under me: and I say to this [man], Go, and he goeth; and to another, Come, and he cometh; and to my servant, Do this, and he doeth it. 8:10 When Jesus heard this, he was amazed at him, and turning to the crowd following him, he said, 8:11"Lookee here! An IMPORTANT guy. Go there. Come here. Do this. Do that. 8:11 Tell you what, Mr. Important Centurion, go check your servant." 8:12 Then the men who had been sent returned to the house and found the servant dead. 8:13 "NOW who's the important guy," Jesus said. 8:14 And when Jesus had come into Peter's house, he saw his wife's mother laid, and sick with a fever. 8:15 And he touched her hand, and the fever left her: and she arose, and ministered to them. Which was good, because who wants a woman with a fever ministering to them? Not Jesus, I can tell you. 8:16 When the evening was come, they brought to him many that were possessed with demons: and he cast out the spirits with word, and healed all that were sick, collecting his 30 drachmas from each (or were they shekels? It's hard to remember); 8:17 That it might be fulfilled which was spoken by Isaiah the prophet, saying, He himself took our infirmities, and bore our sicknesses for a reasonable fee (if 30 shekels or drachmas – whichever – can be called "reasonable"). 8:18 Now when Jesus saw great multitudes about him, he gave a commandment to depart to the other side. 8:19 And a certain scribe came, and said to him, Master, I will follow thee whithersoever thou goest. 8:20 And Jesus saith to him, "Blah, blah, blah! The foxes have holes, and the birds of the air have nests; but the Son of man hath not where to lay his sleepy head. 8:21 And another of his disciples said to him, Lord, suffer me first to go and bury my father. Then you can have HIS bed. 8:22 But Jesus said to him, Follow me; and let the dead bury their dead. ("Nice guy we have for a messiah," a disciple who shall remain nameless whispered to another. "Won't even let poor Obediah bury his dad.") 8:23 And when he had entered into a boat, his disciples followed him. 8:24 And behold, there arose a great tempest in the sea, insomuch that the boat was covered with the waves: but he was asleep. 8:25 And his disciples came to him, and awoke him, saying, Lord, are you NUTS? Sleeping through a tempest such as this? Good God! Save us before we perish. 8:26 And he saith to them, Why are ye fearful, O ye of little faith? Then he arose, scratched his hind quarters, yawned, and rebuked the winds and the sea; and there was a great calm. 8:27 But the men marveled, saying, What manner of man is this, that even the winds and the sea obey him! Cool! 8:28 And when he had come to the other side, into the country of the Gergesenes (not THOSE Gergesenes, but their cousins), there met him two possessed with demons, coming out of the tombs, exceeding fierce, so that no man might pass by that way. 8:29 And behold, they cried out, saying, What have we to do with thee, Jesus, you Son of God you? Art thou come hither (or is it "thither"?) to torment us before the time? 8:30 And there was a good way off from them a herd of many swine, feeding. Which really makes you wonder, since Jews don't eat pork. Can't touch the stuff. God said so. It's like poison to them. 8:31 So the demons besought him, saying,

If thou expellest us, suffer us to go away into the herd of swine. 8:32 And he said to them, Whatever. And when they had come out, they went into the herd of swine: and behold, the whole herd of swine ran violently down a steep place into the sea, and perished in the waters. "Didn't see THAT one coming," Jesus chuckled. 8:33 And they that kept the swine, fled, and went into the city, and told every thing; and what had befallen to the men possessed with demons. 8:34 And behold, the whole city came out to meet Jesus: and when they saw him, they besought him that he would depart out of their borders, so fond of they of demons and swine.

Matthew 9

9:1 And he entered into a boat, and passed over, and came into his own city. 9:2 And behold, they brought to him a man sick with the palsy, lying on a bed: and Jesus, seeing their faith, said to the sick of the palsy, Son, be of good cheer; thy sins are forgiven thee. "Sin? What sin did I commit that caused me to deserve this affliction?" "Your SIN is FORGIVEN," Jesus answered through gritted teeth. "Now get up, for over 30 drachmas, and beat it!" 9:3 And behold, certain of the scribes said within themselves, This man blasphemeth. 9:4 And Jesus, knowing their thoughts, said, Why think ye evil in your hearts? 9:5 For which is easier, to say, Thy sins are forgiven thee; or to say, Arise, and walk? The Pharisees considered it for a moment and said, "The second one only has four syllables while the first one has seven."9:6 Jesus ignored the reply and said, But that ye may know that the Son of man hath power on earth to forgive sins, (then saith he to the sick with the palsy,) "I thought I TOLD thee, Arise, take up thy bed, and go to thy house. Before I get sore! 9:7 And he arose, and departed to his house. 9:8 But when the multitude saw it, they marveled, and glorified God, who had given such power to men. 9:9 And as Jesus was passing from thence, he saw a man named Matthew (cough-cough), sitting at the receipt of custom: and he saith to him, Follow me. And he arose, and followed him, becoming Jesus' FAVORITE apostle of all time. 9:10 And it came to pass, as

Jesus sat at table in the house, behold, many publicans and sinners came and sat down with him and his disciples. 9:11 And when the Pharisees saw it, they said to his disciples, Why eateth your Master with publicans and sinners? 9:12 But when Jesus heard that, he said to them, They that are in health need not a physician, but they that are sick. 9:13 But go ye and learn what that meaneth, dumbasses, I will have mercy, and not sacrifice: for I am not come to call the righteous, but sinners to repentance. And if I make a few drachmas (or shekels, whatever), then what of it? A man's gotta make a living! 9:14

Then came to him the disciples of John, saying, Why do we and the Pharisees fast often, but thy disciples fast not? 9:15 And Jesus said to them, I don't know. Maybe you're just stupid. Then he rolled his eye, sighed and said, Can the children of the bride-chamber mourn, as long as the bridegroom is with them? But the days will come, when the bridegroom shall be taken from them, and then they will fast. 9:16 No man putteth a piece of new cloth to an old garment: for that which is put in to fill it up, taketh from the garment, and the rent is made worse. 9:17 Neither do men put new wine into old bottles: else the bottles break, and the wine runneth out, and the bottles perish: but they put new wine into new bottles, and both are preserved. And the followers of John the Baptist said to themselves as they departed, "This is the guy we were told was coming? What a jerk!" 9:18 While he was saying this, a synagogue leader came and knelt before him and said, "My daughter has just died. But come and put your hand on her, and she will live." 9:19 Seeing an opportunity to make some money, Jesus got up and went with him, and so did his disciples. 9:20 Just then a woman who had been subject to bleeding for twelve years came up behind him and touched the edge of his cloak. 9:21 She said to herself, "If I only touch his cloak, I will be healed." 9:22 Jesus turned and saw her. "Hands off the threads, Grandma," he said, "you'll get blood all over me." 9:23 When Jesus entered the synagogue leader's house and saw the noisy crowd and people playing pipes, 9:24 he said, "Go away. The girl is not dead but asleep." But they laughed at him. 9:25 After the crowd had been put outside, he went in and took the girl by the hand, and she got up. 9:26 News of this spread through all that region. Jesus turned to the father and said, "You'll get the bill. If she drops dead again in 30 days, you'll know there was a problem with your check." 9:27 And when Jesus departed thence, two blind men followed him, crying, and saying, Thou son of David, have mercy on us. 9:28 And when he had come into the house, the blind men came to him: and Jesus saith to them, Believe ye that I am able to do this? They said to him, Yes, Lord, would we be crawling on our bellies in the dirt if we didn't? 9:29 Then he touched their eyes, saying, According to your faith, be it to you. 9:30 And their eyes were opened; and Jesus strictly charged them the standard fee, saying, See that no man know about this. 9:31 But they, when they had departed, spread abroad his fame in all that country. And since they disobeyed the Lord, they not only went blind again, their eyes actually exploded in their heads. 9:32 As they went out, behold, they brought to him a dumb man possessed with a demon. 9:33 And when the demon was cast out and the fee was collected, the dumb man spoke, asking for a receipt: and the multitudes marveled, saying, It was never so seen in Israel. 9:34 But the Pharisees said, He casteth out demons, through the prince of the demons. "You're just jealous," Jesus said. 9:35 And Jesus went about all the cities and villages, teaching in their synagogues, and preaching the gospel of the kingdom, and healing every sickness, and every disease among the people, all the while making a tidy profit. 9:36 But when he saw the multitudes, he was moved with compassion on them, because they fainted, and were scattered abroad, as sheep having no shepherd. 9:37 Then saith he to his disciples, The harvest truly is plentiful, but the laborers are few. 9:38 Pray ye therefore the Lord of the harvest, that he will send forth laborers into his harvest. Just make sure their immigration papers are in order, lest thou be in conflict with God's law about hating and fearing foreigners.

Matthew 10

10:1 And when he had called to him his twelve disciples, he sold them franchises to cast out unclean spirits, to cast them out, and to heal all manner of sickness, and all manner of disease, making sure Jesus got 50 percent of the take. The apostles were free, if they wished, to sell franchises themselves, providing that Jesus got his cut off the top. The apostles were free to fleece their own sheep as they saw fit. 10:2 Now the names of the twelve apostles are these; The first, Simon, who is called Peter (depending on his mood), and Andrew his brother; James the son of Zebedee, and John his brother; 10:3 Philip, and Bartholomew; Thomas, and Matthew the publican; James [the son] of Alpheus, and Lebbeus, whose surname was Thaddeus; 10:4 Simon the Canaanite, and Judas Iscariot, who also betrayed him. But we're getting ahead of ourselves. 10:5 These twelve Jesus sent forth, and commanded them, saying, Go not into the way of the Gentiles, and enter ye not into any city of the Samaritans. 10:6 But go rather to the lost sheep of the house of Israel. 10:7 And as ye go, proclaim, saying, The kingdom of heaven is at hand. 10:8 Heal the sick, cleanse the lepers, raise the dead, cast out demons: freely ye have received, freely give your 50 percent vig to the Lord. 10:9 Provide neither gold, nor silver, nor brass in your purses; 10:10 Nor bag for your journey, neither two coats, neither shoes, nor a staff: for the workman is worthy of his food. 10:11 And into whatever city or town ye shall enter, inquire who in it is worthy, and there abide till ye go thence. 10:12 And when ye come into a house, salute it. 10:13 And if the house be worthy, let your peace come upon it: but if it be not worthy, let your peace return to you. 10:14 And whoever shall not receive you, nor hear your words, burn that place to the ground. 10:15 Verily, I say to you, It shall be more tolerable for the land of Sodom and Gomorrah, in the day of judgment, than for that city. 10:16 Behold, I send you forth as wolves in the midst of sheep: be ye therefore wise as serpents, appear harmless as doves and keep your venom hidden. 10:17 But beware of men: for they will deliver you to the councils, and they will scourge you in their synagogues. 10:18 And ye will be brought before governors and kings for my sake, for a testimony against them and the Gentiles. 10:19 But when they deliver you up, be not anxious how or what ye shall speak, for it shall be given to you in that same hour what ye shall speak. 10:20 For it is not ye that speak, but the Spirit of your Father which speaketh in you. 10:21 And the brother will deliver up the brother to death, and the father the child: and the children will rise up against their parents, and cause them to be put to death. 10:22 And ye will be hated by all men for my name's sake: but he that endureth to the end shall be saved. 10:23 But when they persecute you in this city, flee ye into another after you've destroyed the hateful place: for verily I say to you, Ye shall not have gone over the cities of Israel till the Son of man shall have come. 10:24 The disciple is not above his teacher, nor the servant above his lord. 10:25 It is enough for the disciple that he should be as his teacher, and the servant as his lord: if they have called the master of the house Beelzebub, how much more will they call them of his household? 10:26 Fear them not therefore: for there is nothing covered, that shall not be revealed; and hid, that shall not be known. 10:27 What I tell you in darkness, that speak ye in light: and what ye hear in the ear, that publish ye upon the housetops. 10:28 And fear not them who kill the body, but are not able to kill the soul: but rather fear him who is able to destroy both soul and body in hell. 10:29 Are not two sparrows sold for a farthing? and not one of them shall fall on the ground without your Father. 10:30 But the very hairs of your head are all numbered. 10:31 Fear ye not therefore, ye are of more value than many sparrows. I would place the number at nine. You are each worth nine sparrows in the eyes of your lord. 10:32 Whoever therefore shall confess me before men, him will I also confess before my Father who is in heaven. 10:33 But whoever shall deny me before men, him will I also deny before my Father who is in heaven. 10:34 Think not that I am come to send peace on earth: I came not to send peace, but a sword. 10:35 For I am come to set a man at variance against his father, and the daughter against her mother, and the daughter-in-law against her mother-in-law (not that that would be all that difficult). 10:36 And a man's foes will be they of his own household. 10:37 He that loveth father or mother more than me, is not worthy of me: and he that loveth son or daughter more than me, is not worthy of me. 10:38 And he that taketh not his cross, and followeth me, is not worthy of me. 10:39 He that findeth his life shall lose it: and he that loseth his life for my sake, shall find it. 10:40 He that receiveth you, receiveth me, and he that receiveth me, receiveth him that sent me. 10:41 He that receiveth a prophet in the name of a prophet, shall receive a prophet's reward; and he that receiveth a righteous man in the name of a righteous man, shall receive a righteous man's reward. 10:42 And whoever shall give to drink to one of these little ones, a cup of cold water only, in the name of a disciple, verily, I say to you, he shall in no wise lose his reward. Just make sure you get paid for the water. Water isn't free. The disciples were astonished at these pronouncements. "Who peed in his morning grain," Simon who was sometimes called Peter asked Andrew.

Matthew 11

11:1 And it came to pass when Jesus had made an end of bossing around his twelve disciples, he departed thence to teach and to preach and annoy in their cities. 11:2 Now when his nutbag cousin John had heard in the prison the works of Christ, he sent two of his disciples, 11:3 And said to him, Art thou he that should come, or do we look for another? 11:4 Jesus answered and said to them, Go and show John again those things which ye hear and see: 11:5 The blind receive their sight, and the lame walk, the lepers are cleansed, and the deaf hear, the dead are raised, and the poor have the gospel preached to them. 11:6 And blessed is he to whom I shall not be the cause of his falling into sin. Could you come and tell him yourself, John's disciples asked. "He's been asking for you, and…" "Goodness, look at the time," Jesus said cutting them off. 11:7 And as they departed, Jesus began to say to the multitudes concerning his stinky cousin John, What went ye out into the wilderness to see? A reed shaken with the wind? 11:8 But what went ye out to see? A man clothed in soft raiment? Behold, they that wear soft clothing are in kings' houses. 11:9 But what went ye out to see? A prophet? Yes, I say to you, and more than a prophet. 11:10 For this is he concerning whom it is written, Behold, I send my messenger before thy face, who shall prepare thy way before thee. 11:11 Verily, I say to you, among them that are born of women, there hath not risen a greater than John the Baptist: notwithstanding, he that is least in the kingdom of heaven, is greater than he. Confused yet? Good. 11:12 And from the days of John the Baptist, until now, the kingdom of heaven suffereth violence, and the violent take it by force. 11:13 For all the prophets and the law prophesied until John. 11:14 And if ye will receive it, this is Elijah who was to come. 11:15 He that hath ears to hear, let him hear. 11:16 But to what shall I liken this generation? It is like to children, sitting in the markets, and calling to their fellows, 11:17 And saying, We have piped to you, and ye have not danced; We have mourned to you, and ye have not lamented. 11:18 For John came neither eating nor drinking, and they say, He hath a demon. 11:19 The Son of man came eating and drinking, and they say, Behold, a man gluttonous, and a wine-bibber, a friend of publicans and sinners. But wisdom is justified by her children. 11:20 Then he began to upbraid the cities in which most of his mighty works had been done, because they repented not. 11:21 Woe to thee, Chorazin; woe to thee, Bethsaida: for if the mighty works which have been done in you had been done in Tyre and Sidon, they would have repented long ago in sackcloth and ashes. 11:22 But I say to you, It shall be more tolerable for Tyre and Sidon at the day of judgment, than for you. 11:23 And thou, Capernaum, which art exalted to heaven, shalt be brought down to hell: for if the mighty works which have been done in thee, had been done in Sodom, it would have remained until this day. 11:24 But I say to you, that it shall be more tolerable for the land of Sodom, in the day of judgment, than for thee. One of his disciples spoke up, saying, "Maybe we need to do a better job scouting these cities before we go there." 11:25 At that time Jesus answered and said, I thank thee, O Father, Lord of heaven and earth, because thou hast hid these things from the wise and prudent, and hast revealed them to babes. 11:26 Even so, Father, for so it seemed good in thy sight. 11:27 All things are delivered to me by my Father; and no man knoweth the Son, but the Father; neither knoweth any man the Father, save the Son, and he to whomsoever the Son will reveal him. 11:28 Come to me, all ye that profit from the labor of others, and are heavy laden with taxes, and I will give you relief from your burden. 11:29 Take my yoke upon you, and learn from me: for I am meek and lowly in heart; and ye shall find rest to your souls. 11:30 For my yoke is easy, and my tax rate is a flat 15 percent.

Matthew 12

12:1 At that time Jesus went on the Sabbath through the corn, and his disciples were hungry, and began to pluck the ears of corn, and to eat. 12:2 But when the Pharisees saw it, they said to him, Behold, thy disciples do that which it is not lawful to do on the Sabbath. Actually, stealing corn is illegal EVERY day, but especially on the Sabbath. 12:3 But he said to them, Have ye not read what David did when he was hungry, and they that were with him; 12:4 How he entered into the house of God, and ate the show-bread, which it was not lawful for him to eat, neither for them who were with him, but only for the priests? 12:5 Or have ye not read in the law, that on the Sabbath the priests in the temple profane the Sabbath, and are blameless? 12:6 But I say to you, that in this place is one greater than the temple. 12:7 But if ye had known what this meaneth, I will have mercy, and not sacrifice, ye would not have condemned the guiltless. 12:8 For the Son of man is Lord even of the Sabbath.

The Pharisees looked at each other, shaking their heads and shrugging their shoulders. The disciples looked at their sandal tips and said nothing. 12:9 Going on from that place, he went into their synagogue, 12:10 and a man with a shriveled hand was there. Looking for a reason to bring charges against Jesus, they asked him, "Is it lawful to heal on the Sabbath?" 12:11 He said to them, "If any of you see a shekel laying on the road on the Sabbath, would you not bend over to pick it up? 12:12 I get 30 shekels per miracle! Therefore it is lawful to make a buck on the Sabbath." 12:13 Then he said to the man, "Stretch out your hand." So he stretched it out and it was completely restored, just as sound as the other. "That will be 30 shekels," Jesus said. "You have 30 days to pony up, or the hand turns back into a claw." Peter wrote down an address for the man so he could send the payment 12:14 Then the Pharisees went out, and held a council against him, how they might destroy him. 12:15 But when Jesus knew it, he withdrew himself from thence: and great multitudes followed him, and he healed them all – 30 denarii a head. See, he decided to settle on a single currency from this point to avoid the whole "shekel vs. drachma controversy. 12:16 And charged them that they should not make him known: 12:17 That it might be fulfilled which was spoken by Isaiah the prophet, saying, 12:18 Behold, my servant, whom I have chosen; my beloved, in whom my soul is well pleased: I will put my spirit upon him, and he shall show judgment to the Gentiles. 12:19 He shall not contend, nor cry; neither shall any man hear his voice in the streets. 12:20 A bruised reed shall he not break, and smoking flax shall he not quench, till he shall send forth judgment to victory. 12:21 And in his name shall the Gentiles trust. And the disciples took the multitudes out of Jesus' earshot and told them, "Yes, he rambles. But look at the good he does. And for such a low price!" 12:22 Then was brought to him one possessed with a demon, blind and dumb; and he healed him, so that the blind and dumb both spoke and saw. Later, when he was tired, he accidentally made a blind man walk and a cripple see. He realized his error and charged them half-price. 12:23 And all the people were amazed, and said, Is not this the son of David? 12:24 But when the Pharisees heard it, they said, This doth not cast out demons, but by Beelzebub the prince of the demons. The Pharisees never had anything nice to say about anyone. 12:25 And Jesus knew their thoughts, and said to them, Every kingdom divided against itself, is brought to desolation; and every city or house divided against itself, shall not stand. 12:26 And if Satan casteth out Satan, he is divided against himself; how then shall his kingdom stand? 12:27 And if I by Beelzebub cast out demons, by whom do your children expel them? Therefore they shall be your judges. 12:28 But if I cast out demons by the Spirit of God, then the kingdom of God is come to you. 12:29 Or else, how can one enter into a strong man's house, and seize his goods, except he shall first bind the strong man? and then he will plunder his house. 12:30 He that is not with me, is against me; and he that gathereth not with me, scattereth abroad. 12:31 Wherefore I say to you, All manner of sin and blasphemy shall be forgiven to men: but the blasphemy against the Holy Spirit shall not be forgiven to men. 12:32 And whoever speaketh a word against the Son of man, it shall be forgiven him: but whoever speaketh against the Holy Spirit, it shall not be forgiven him, neither in this world, neither in the world to come. So watch your mouths! 12:33 Either make the tree good, and its fruit good; or else make the tree corrupt, and its fruit corrupt: for the tree is known by its fruit. 12:34 O generation of vipers, how can ye, being evil, speak good things? For out of the abundance of the heart, the mouth speaketh. The Pharisees began to shift restlessly as they nudged each other whispering, "See what you've done? You got him started." 12:35 Jesus continued his rant. "A good man, out of the good treasure of the heart, bringeth forth good things: and an evil man, out of the evil treasure, bringeth forth evil things. 12:36 But I say to you, that for every idle word that men shall speak, they shall give account in the day of judgment. If they have good REASON for saying the evil things, they shall enter the kingdom. 12:37 For by thy words thou shalt be justified, and by thy words thou shalt be condemned. 12:38 Then certain of the scribes and of the Pharisees who didn't know to leave well enough alone, answered, saying, Master, we would see a sign from thee. 12:39 But he answered and said to them, An evil and adulterous generation seeketh for a sign, and there shall no sign be given to it, but the sign of the prophet Jonah. 12:40 For as Jonah was three days and three nights in the whale's belly: so shall the Son of man be three days and three nights in the heart of the earth. 12:41 The men of Nineveh shall rise in judgment with this generation, and shall condemn it: because they repented at the preaching of Jonah; and behold, a greater than Jonah is here. 12:42 The queen of the south shall rise up in the judgment with this generation, and shall condemn it: for she came from the uttermost parts of the earth to hear the wisdom of Solomon; and behold, a greater than Solomon is here. 12:43 When the unclean spirit is gone out of a man, he walketh through dry places, seeking rest, and he findeth none. 12:44 Then he saith, I will return into my house from whence I came out; and when he is come, he findeth it empty, swept, and garnished. 12:45 Then goeth he, and taketh with himself seven other spirits more wicked than himself, and they enter in and dwell there: and the last state of that man is worse than the first. Even so shall it be also to this wicked generation. The Pharisees opened and closed their mouths wordlessly as several of the Apostles told them, "It's all right. We don't know what the hell he's talking about half the time either." 12:46 While he was yet speaking to the people, behold, his mother and his brethren stood without, desiring to speak with him. She desired to drag him home by his beard and start working some of these miracles around the house. Joseph had since died (or so the suicide note said, although no body was ever found) and there was stuff needing doing around the homestead in Nazareth. 12:47 Then one said to him, Behold, thy mother and thy brethren stand without, desiring to speak with thee. 12:48 But he answered and said to him that told him, Who is my mother? And who are my brethren? 12:49 And he stretched forth his hand towards his disciples, and said, Behold my mother and my brethren! 12:50 For whoever shall do the will of my Father who is in heaven, the same is my brother, and sister, and mother. "Just don't come calling me when the Romans nail you to a tree," his mother shouted as his brothers dragged her away.

Matthew 13

13:1 The same day Jesus went out of the house, and sat by the seaside. 13:2 And great multitudes were gathered to him and bad was their collective stench, so that he went into a boat, and sat down; and the whole multitude stood on the shore. 13:3 And he spoke many things to them in parables, saying, Behold, a sower went forth to sow; 13:4 And when he sowed, some seeds fell by the way side, and the fowls came and devoured them: 13:5 Some fell upon stony places, where they had not much earth: and forthwith they sprung up, because they had no deepness of earth: 13:6 And when the sun had risen, they were scorched; and because they had not root, they withered. 13:7 And some fell among thorns; and the thorns sprung up, and choked them: 13:8 But others fell into good ground, and brought forth fruit, some a hundred-fold, some sixty-fold, some thirty-fold. 13:9 Who hath ears to hear, let him hear. 13:10 And the disciples came, and said to him, Why speakest thou to them in parables? These people aren't idiots. They know you can't plant crops in stony soil. A little show of respect from you would go a long way with these folks. You've been such a pill lately. And man, is your mom pissed at you! 13:11 He answered and said to them, Because it is given to you to know the mysteries of the kingdom of heaven, but to them it is not given. 13:12 For whoever hath, to him shall be given, and he shall have more abundance: but whoever hath not, from him shall be taken away even that which he hath. 13:13 Therefore I speak to them in parables: because they seeing see not; and hearing they hear not, neither do they understand. 13:14 And in them is fulfilled the prophecy of Isaiah, which saith, Those who got will get more. Those who do not will get nothing. This is the law of the Lord. 13:15 For this people's heart is become gross, and their ears are dull of hearing, and their eyes they have closed; lest at any time they should see with eyes, and hear with their ears, and should understand with their heart, and should be converted, and I should heal them. 13:16 But blessed are your eyes, for they see: and your ears, for they hear. 13:17 For verily I say to you, That many prophets and righteous have desired to see the things which ye see, and have not seen them and to hear the things which ye hear, and have not heard them. 13:18 The disciples, their asses sufficiently kissed, were in a more agreeable mood. "OK, it's story time," Jesus said. "Hear ye therefore the parable of the sower. 13:19 When any one heareth the word of the kingdom, and understandeth it not, then cometh the wicked one and catcheth away that which was sown in his heart. This is he who received seed by the way side. 13:20 But he that received the seed into stony places, the same is he that heareth the word, and immediately with joy receiveth it; 13:21 Yet he hath not root in himself, but endureth for a while: for when tribulation or persecution ariseth because of the word, forthwith he is offended. 13:22 He also that received seed among the thorns is he that heareth the word; and the care of this world, and the deceitfulness of trying to improve the condition of the world choke the word, and he becometh unfruitful. 13:23 But he that receiveth seed into the good ground is he that heareth the word, and understandeth; who also beareth fruit, and bringeth forth, some a hundred fold, some sixty, some thirty. 13:24 Another parable he proposed to them, saying, The kingdom of heaven is likened to a man who sowed good seed in his field: 13:25 But while men slept, his enemy came and sowed tares among the wheat, and departed – the bastard! 13:26 But when the blade had sprung up, and brought forth fruit, then appeared the tares also. 13:27 So the servants of the householder came and said to him, Sir, didst thou not sow good seed in thy field? From whence then hath it tares? 13:28 He said to them, An enemy hath done this. The servants said to him, Wilt thou then that we go and gather our enemies and shove the tares up their hiney holes? 13:29 But he said, No; lest while ye gather the tares, ye root up also the wheat with them. 13:30 Let both grow together until the harvest: and in the time of harvest I will say to the reapers,

Gather ye first the tares, and bind them in bundles to shove up the hiney holes of my enemies: but gather the wheat into my barn. 13:31 Another parable he proposed to them, saying, The kingdom of heaven is like a grain of mustard-seed, which a man took, and sowed in his field: 13:32 Which indeed is the least of all seeds: but when it is grown, it is the greatest among herbs, and becometh a tree, so that the birds of the air come and lodge on its branches. I like mustard. Don't you? 13:33 Another parable he spoke to them; The kingdom of heaven is like leaven, which a woman took, and hid in three measures of meal, till the whole was leavened. 13:34 All these things Jesus spoke to the multitude in parables; and without a parable he spoke not to them so that they wondered about his sanity: 13:35 That it might be fulfilled which was spoken by the prophet, saying, I will open my mouth in parables; I will utter things which have been kept secret from the foundation of the world. 13:36 Then Jesus sent the multitude away, and went into the house: and his disciples came to him, saying, Declare to us the parable of the tares of the field. We want a story before we go to sleep. 13:37 He answered and said to them, He that soweth the good seed is the Son of man; 13:38 The field is the world; the good seed are the children of the kingdom; but the tares are the children of the wicked one. 13:39 The enemy that sowed them is the devil; the harvest is the end of the world; and the reapers are the angels. 13:40 As therefore the tares are gathered and shoved up the hiney holes of the wicked; so shall it be in the end of this world. 13:41 The Son of man shall send forth his angels, and they shall gather out of his kingdom all things that offend, and them who do iniquity; 13:42 And shall shove them into a hiney hole of fire: there shall be wailing and gnashing of teeth. 13:43 Then shall the righteous shine as the sun in the kingdom of their Father. Who hath ears to hear, let him hear. 13:44 Again, the kingdom of heaven is like treasure hid in a field; which, when a man hath found, he hideth, and for joy hereof goeth and selleth all that he hath, and buyeth that field. 13:45 Again, the kingdom of heaven is like a merchant seeking goodly pearls: 13:46 Who, when he had found one pearl of great price, went and sold all that he had, and bought it. 13:47 Again, the kingdom of heaven is like a net, that was cast into the sea, and gathered of every kind: 13:48 Which, when it was full, they drew to the shore, and sat down, and gathered the good into vessels, but cast away the bad. 13:49 So shall it be at the end of the world: the angels shall come forth, and sever the wicked from among the just, 13:50 And shall cast them into the furnace of fire: there shall be wailing and gnashing of teeth. 13:51 Jesus saith to them, Have ye understood all these things? They say to him, Yes, Lord. Such liars were they. 13:52 Then said he to them, Therefore every scribe who is instructed to the kingdom of heaven, is like a man that is a householder, who bringeth forth out of his treasures new and old. 13:53 And it came to pass, that when Jesus had finished these parables, he departed thence. 13:54 And when he had come into his own country, he taught them in their synagogue, so that they were astonished, and said, Whence hath this this wisdom, and mighty works? 13:55 Is not this the carpenter's son? Is not his mother called Mary? And his brethren, James, and Joses, and Simon, and Judas? 13:56 And his sisters whose names we can't remember, are they not all with us? Whence then hath this man all these things? 13:57 And they were offended in him. But Jesus said to them, A prophet is not without honor, save in his own country, and in his own house. 13:58 He told them to fornicate with themselves and departed.

Matthew 14

14:1 At that time Herod the Tetrarch heard of the fame of Jesus, 14:2 And said to his servants, This is John the Baptist; he hath risen from the dead; and therefore mighty works do show forth themselves in him. 14:3 For Herod had laid hold on John, and bound him, and put him in prison for the sake of Herodias, his brother Philip's wife. 14:4 For John had said to him, It is not lawful for thee to have her. 14:5 And when he would have put him to death, he feared the multitude, because they counted him as a prophet. 14:6 But when Herod's birthday was kept, the

daughter of Herodias danced before them, and pleased Herod. 14:7 Upon which he promised with an oath to give her whatever she would ask. 14:8 And she, being before instructed by her mother, said, Give me here the head of John the Baptist in a dish. 14:9 And the king was sorry: nevertheless for the sake of the oath, and of them who sat with him at table, he commanded it to be given her.   14:10 And he sent, and beheaded John in the prison. 14:11 And his head was brought in a dish, and given to the damsel: and she brought it to her mother. 14:12 And his disciples came, and took up the body, and buried it, and went and told Jesus. 14:13 When Jesus heard of it, he smacked himself of the forehead. "Right! John! I kept MEANING to get him out of jail. Oh well." He departed thence in a boat, into a desert place apart: and when the people had heard of it they followed him on foot out of the cities. 14:14 And Jesus went forth, and saw a great multitude, and was moved with profit motive towards them, and he healed their sick and raked in the dinarii. 14:15 One of the disciples said, `A boy here has five loaves of bread and two small fish. But what can that little bit of food do for so many people?' 14:16 Jesus rolled his eyes, sighed and said, `Tell the people to sit down.' Much grass was there and much had been smoked, so naturally the people were very, very hungry and willing to eat anything, even raw fish and bread. The number of men who sat down was about five thousand. Then Jesus took the bread from the little boy without paying him for it and thanked God for the fact that little children are easy to bully. He gave it to the disciples and they divided it among those who were sitting. He did the same thing with the fish. The people had all they wanted. 14:17 When they had eaten enough, he said to his disciples, `Gather up all the pieces that are left so that nothing will be lost. I'm not made of fish and bread.' 14:18 They gathered all the pieces of the five loaves. Twelve baskets full were left over after all the people had eaten enough. 14:19 When those men saw the big work that Jesus did, they said, `Truly, this is the Prophet that is to come into the world.' 14:20 The people wanted to take Jesus by force to make him a king. When he saw this, he left again and went on the hill by himself. 14:21 "Bloody leeches," he was heard murmuring as he walked away. 14:22 And immediately Jesus constrained his disciples to get into a boat, and to go before him to the other side, while he sent the multitudes away. 14:23 And when he had sent the multitudes away, he ascended a mountain apart to pray: and when the evening was come, he was there alone. 14:24 But the boat was now in the midst of the sea, tossed with waves: for the wind was contrary. 14:25 And in the fourth watch of the night Jesus went to them, walking on the sea. 14:26 And when the disciples saw him walking on the sea, they were troubled, saying, It is a spirit; and they cried out for fear. 14:27 But immediately Jesus spoke to them, saying, Be of good cheer; it is I; be not afraid. 14:28 And Peter answered him and said, Lord, if it is thou, bid me come to thee on the water. 14:29 And he said, Come. And when Peter had come down out of the boat, he sank like a rock. 14:30 Jesus took a few moments to let Peter realize the seriousness of his situation. 14:31 Then Jesus stretched forth his hand, and caught him, and said to him, What lesson have we learned here? Peter could not speak, as his windpipe was filled with water. "What we have LEARNED here, Peter, is that ONE of is the Son of Man, and one of us is NOT. Savvy?" Peter nodded, choking and spitting and got back into the boat. 14:32 And when they had come into the boat, the wind ceased. 14:33 Then they that were in the boat came and worshiped him, saying, In truth thou art the son of God. 14:34 And when they had gone over, they came into the land of Gennesaret. 14:35 And when the men of that place had knowledge of him, they sent out into all the surrounding country, and brought to him all that were diseased; 14:36 And besought him that they might only touch the hem of his garment: and as many as touched were restored to health. Many denarii were made that night, I can tell you.

Matthew 15

15:1 Then came to Jesus scribes and Pharisees, who were of Jerusalem, saying, 15:2 Why do thy disciples transgress the tradition of the elders? For they wash not their hands when they eat bread. 15:3 But he answered and said to them, Why do ye also transgress the commandment of God by your tradition? 15:4 For God commanded, saying, "Mind Your Own Damn Business!" and, while we're at it, "He that curseth father or mother, let him die the death. 15:5 But ye say, Whoever shall say to his father or mother, it is a gift, by whatever thou mightest be profited by me; 15:6 And honor not his father or his mother, he shall be free. Thus have ye made the commandment of God of no effect by your tradition. The Pharisees said, "Huh?" 15:7 Jesus rose to his feet and clenched his fists. Ye hypocrites, well did Isaiah prophesy of you, saying, 15:8 This people draw nigh to me with their mouth, and honor me with their lips; but their heart is far from me. 15:9 But in vain they do worship me, teaching for doctrines the commandments of men. 15:10 And he called the multitude, and said to them, Hear, and understand: 15:11 Not that which goeth into the mouth defileth a man – within certain limits, of course; but that which cometh out of the mouth, this defileth a man. 15:12 Then came his disciples, and said to him, Knowest thou that the Pharisees were offended after they heard this saying? 15:13 But he answered and said, "Screw them. Every plant, which my heavenly Father hath not planted, shall be extirpated. 15:14 Let them alone: they are blind leaders of the blind. And if the blind leadeth the blind, both will fall into the ditch. And there will be much laughing and pointing. 15:15 Then answered Peter and said to him, Declare to us this parable. 15:16 And Jesus said, Story time again, eh? Are ye also yet without understanding? 15:17 Do ye not yet understand, that whatever entereth in at the mouth goeth into the belly, and is cast out into the crapper? 15:18 But those things which proceed out of the mouth come forth from the heart; and they defile the man. 15:19 For out of the heart proceed evil thoughts, murders, adulteries, fornications, thefts, false witness, blasphemies: 15:20 These are [the things] which defile a man: but to eat with unwashen hands defileth not a man. It's just gross, is all. I mean, look at your fingernails. They're disgusting. 15:21 Then Jesus went thence, and departed into the territories of Tyre and Sidon. 15:22 And behold, a woman of Canaan came out of the same territories, and cried to him, saying, Have mercy on me, O Lord, thou son of David; my daughter is grievously afflicted with a demon. 15:23 But he answered her not a word. And his disciples came and besought him, saying, Send her away; for she crieth after us. 15:24 But he answered and said, I am not sent but to the lost sheep of the house of Israel. 15:25 Then came she and worshiped him,

saying, Lord, help me. 15:26 But he answered and said, It is not meet to take the children's bread, and to cast it to dogs. 15:27 And she said, Truth, Lord, I've heard you were a mystic and not the easiest guy to get a yes or no answer from: yet the dogs eat of the crumbs which fall from their master's table. 15:28 Then Jesus answered and said to her, Awwww... you're good to your doggies! O woman, great is thy faith: be it to thee even as thou wilt. And give your doggies a hug for me. And her daughter was healed from that very hour. 15:29 And Jesus departed from thence, and came nigh to the sea of Galilee; and ascended a mountain, and sat down there. 15:30 And great multitudes came to him, having with them those that were lame, blind, dumb, maimed, and many others, and cast them down at Jesus' feet; and he healed them, collecting his customary fee or a promissory note from those who could not pay just then with the warning that the affliction would return in force after 30 days if the bill went unpaid. 15:31 So that the multitude wondered, when they saw the dumb to speak, the maimed to be whole, the lame to walk, and the blind to see: and they glorified the God of Israel. 15:32 Then Jesus called his disciples to him and said, I have compassion on the multitude, because they continue with me now three days, and have nothing to eat: and I will not send them away fasting, lest they faint in the way. 15:33 And his disciples said to him, Whence should we have so much bread in the wilderness, as to satisfy so great a multitude? 15:34 And Jesus saith to them, I guess I have to do the bread and fish thing again. How many loaves have ye? And they said, Seven, and a few little fishes. 15:35 And he commanded the multitude to sit on the ground. 15:36 And he took the seven loaves and the fishes, and gave thanks, and broke them, and gave to his disciples, and the disciples to the multitude. 15:37 And they all ate and were filled: and they took up of the fragments that were left seven baskets full. 15:38 And they that had eaten were four thousand men, besides women and children. 15:39 And he sent away the multitude, and took a boat, and came into the borders of Magdala. Peter turned to Matthew and said, didn't this happen just a chapter ago. Matthew bade Peter to shut his fish hole.

Matthew 16

16:1 The Pharisees also and the Sadducees came, and, tempting, desired him that he would show them a sign from heaven. 16:2 He answered and said to them, When it is evening, ye say, It will be fair weather: for the sky is red. 16:3 And in the morning, It will be foul weather today: for the sky is red and lowering. Right, the Pharisees said. "Red sky at morning, sailor take warning. Red sky at night, sailor's delight." They chuckled at their witty saying. Jesus was not amused. O ye hypocrites, ye can discern the face of the sky; but can ye not discern the signs of the times? 16:4 A wicked and adulterous generation seeketh for a sign; and there shall no sign been to it, but the sign of the prophet Jonah. And he left them, and departed. "Oh, right… Jonah and the whale again. I guess he's going to get eaten by a fish or something. And THAT'LL show us?" Whereupon they departed for their weekly Pharisee meeting. 16:5 And when his disciples had come to the other side, they had forgotten to take bread. 16:6 Then Jesus said to them, Take heed and beware of the leaven of the Pharisees and of the Sadducees. 16:7 And they reasoned among themselves, saying, It is because we have taken no bread. 16:8 Which when Jesus perceived, he said to them, O ye of little faith, why reason ye among yourselves, because ye have brought no bread? 16:9 Do ye not yet understand, neither remember the five loaves of the five thousand, and how many baskets ye took up? 16:10 Neither the seven loaves of the four thousand, and how many baskets ye took up? 16:11 How is it that ye do not understand that I spoke not to you concerning bread, that ye should beware of the leaven of the Pharisees and of the Sadducees? 16:12 Then they understood that he did not caution them against the leaven of bread, but against the doctrine of the Pharisees and of the Sadducees. "Yeah, but how does that fix the problem of our forgetting to bring any bread," Andrew asked. Jesus smacked him on the forehead with an open palm. 16:13 When Jesus came into the borders of Cesarea Phillippi, he asked his disciples, saying, Who do men say that I the Son of man is? 16:14 And they said, Some say that thou art John the Baptist: some Elijah; and others, Jeremiah, or one of the prophets. 16:15 He saith to them, But who say ye that I am? 16:16 And Simon Peter answered and said, Thou art the Christ, the Son of the living God. 16:17 And Jesus answered and said to him, Blessed art thou, Simon-Barjona: for flesh and blood hath not revealed it to thee, but my Father who is in heaven. 16:18 And I say also to thee, that thou art Peter, and upon this rock I will build my church: and the gates of hell shall not prevail against it. 16:19 And I will give to thee the keys of the kingdom of heaven: and whatever thou shalt bind on earth, shall be bound in heaven; and whatever thou shalt loose on earth, shall be loosed in heaven. 16:20 Then he charged his disciples that they should tell no man that he was Jesus the Christ. Peter turned to Judas and said, "Guess who's the pope NOW!" Judas seemed troubled. But he was always like that. 16:21 From that time forth Jesus began to show to his disciples, that he must go to Jerusalem, and suffer many things from the elders and chief priests, and scribes, and be killed, and be raised again the third day. 16:22 Then Peter took him, and began to rebuke him, saying, Be it far from thee, Lord: this shall not be to thee. 16:23 But he turned, and said to Peter, Get thee behind me, Satan; thou art an offense to me: for thou savorest not the things that are of God, but those that are of men. "Satan," Peter said to Judas? Earlier I was the rock of his church, now I make a simple statement and I'm Satan! Hell of a thing to say to the new pope. Judas still appeared troubled, but like I said earlier, he usually did. 16:24 Then said Jesus to his disciples, If any man will come after me, let him deny himself, and take up his cross, and follow me. 16:25 For whoever will save his life, shall lose it: and whoever will lose his life for my sake, shall find it. 16:26 For what is a man profited, if he shall gain the whole world, and lose his own soul? or what shall a man give in exchange for his soul? 16:27 For the Son of man will come in the glory of his Father, with his angels; and then he will reward every man according to his works. 16:28 Verily I say to you, There are some standing here, who shall not taste death, till they shall see the Son of man coming in his kingdom. "Does anyone here have any idea what the hell he's talking about," Peter, still smarting from the Satan remark, asked Judas. But Judas remained silent, refusing to make eye contact as was his usual style. On retrospect, someone should have kept an eye on the sneaky bastard. But we're getting ahead of ourselves again.

Matthew 17

17:1 And after six days, Jesus taketh Peter, James, and John his brother, and bringeth them upon a high mountain apart. 17:2 And he was transfigured before them: and his face shone as the sun, and his raiment was white as the light. 17:3 And behold, there appeared to them Moses and Elijah talking with him. 17:4 Then answered Peter, and said to Jesus, Lord, it is good for us to be here and these mushrooms you gave for us to eat a half hour ago are splendid: if thou wilt, let us make here three tabernacles; one for thee, and one for Moses, and one for Elijah. And who knew Elijah had tentacles? 17:5 While he was yet speaking, behold, a bright cloud overshadowed them: and behold, a voice out of the cloud, which said, This is my beloved Son, in whom I am well pleased: hear ye him. (Which means I was mistaken when I wrote earlier that when Jesus got baptized that was the last time anyone actually heard God speak. Note to self: Change that before this gets into the Bible.) 17:6 And when the disciples heard it, they fell on their face, and were in great fear. 17:7 And Jesus came and touched them, and said, Arise, and be not afraid. 17:8 And when they had lifted up their eyes, they saw no man, save Jesus only. Peter rubbed his forehead. "Man, these mushrooms!" 17:9 And as they were descending the mountain, Jesus charged them, saying, Tell the vision to no man, until the Son of man be raised again from the dead. 17:10 And his disciples asked him, saying, Why then say the scribes, that Elijah must first come? 17:11 And Jesus answered and said to them, Elijah truly will first come, and restore all things: 17:12 But I say to you, that Elijah is come already, and they knew him not, but have done to him whatever they pleased: likewise will also the Son of man suffer by them. 17:13 Then the disciples understood that he spoke to them concerning John the Baptist. "Oh, so HE was Elijah! Why didn't he just say…" Andrew said before being smacked on the forehead by the open palm of the Master. 17:14 And when they had come to the multitude, there came to him a certain man kneeling down to him, and saying, 17:15 Lord, have mercy on my son; for he is lunatic, and grievously distressed; for often he falleth into the fire, and often into the water. 17:16 And I brought him to thy disciples, and they could not cure him. 17:17 Then Jesus rolled his eyes and sighed saying, "O faithless and perverse generation, how long shall I be with you? How long shall I suffer you? Bring him hither to me. (Or is it thither?) 17:18 And Jesus rebuked the demon, and he departed out of him: and the child was cured from that very hour. (Really, Luke writes a much better account of this event. I must admit. I wasn't there at the time and am relying on second-hand accounts.) 17:19 Then came the disciples to Jesus apart, and said, Why could not we cast him out? 17:20 And Jesus said to them, Because you are idiots.

Matthew 18

18:1 At the same time came the disciples to Jesus, saying, Who is the greatest in the kingdom of heaven? I say it's you, but James says he thinks it's him. Should I smite James, or do you want to? 18:2 And Jesus called a little child to him, and set him in the midst of them, 18:3 And said, Verily I say to you, Except ye be converted, and become as little children, ye shall not enter into the kingdom of heaven. 18:4 Whoever therefore shall humble himself as this little child, the same is greatest in the kingdom of heaven. 18:5 And whoever shall receive one such little child in my name, receiveth me. 18:6 But whoever shall cause one of these little ones who believe in me, to sin, it were better for him that a millstone were hanged about his neck, and that he were drowned in the depth of the sea. 18:7 Woe to the world because of offenses! For it must needs be that offenses come; but woe to that man by whom the offense cometh! 18:8 At risk of repeating myself, if thy hand or thy foot causeth thee to sin, cut them off, and cast them from thee (or have someone do it for you, I mean, how are you going to "cast" something with no hands?): it is better for thee to enter into life halt or maimed, rather than having two hands or two feet, to be cast into everlasting fire. 18:9 And if thy eye causeth thee to sin, pluck it out, and cast it from thee: it is better for thee to enter into life with one eye, rather than having two eyes, to be cast into hell-fire. 18:10 Take heed that ye despise not one of these little ones: And I'm looking at you, Peter, because you will be the first Pope and you will set the tone for bishops and priests who follow you. If I hear of a scandal in my church with priests harming these little ones in any way, I'm going to be righteously pissed. For I say to you, that in heaven their angels do always behold he face of my Father who is in heaven. 18:11 For the Son of man is come to save that which was lost. 18:12 "What do you think? If a man owns a hundred sheep, and one of them wanders away, will he not leave the ninety-nine on the hills and go to look for the one that wandered off? Maybe. 18:13 And if he finds it, I tell you the truth, he is happier about that one sheep than about the ninety-nine that did not wander off. But when he gets back to the flock and finds the other ninety-nine eaten by wolves, their bones scattered about the field, he will take out his wrath on the little sheep he abandoned his flock to save. He will slaughter that sheep in as painful a manner as possible, skin it while it still lives, wear the wool as the dying sheep regards him, then roast and eat its flesh. 18:14 In the same way your Father in heaven is not willing that any of these little ones should be lost. Just don't think he's going to risk the entire flock to come looking for your ass if you wander away from the other sheep. 18:15 Moreover, if thy brother shall trespass against thee, go and tell him his fault between thee and him alone: if he shall hear thee, thou hast gained thy brother. 18:16 But if he will not hear thee, then take with thee one or two lawyers, that in the mouth of two or three witnesses every word may be established. 18:17 And if he shall neglect to hear them, tell it to the courts: but if he shall neglect to hear the courts, let his ass rot in jail. 18:18 Verily I say to you, Whatever ye shall bind on earth, shall be bound in heaven (unless you can wiggle out on a technicality): and whatever ye shall loose on earth, shall be loosed in heaven. So be careful who you loose. 18:19 Again I say to you, That if two of you shall agree on earth, concerning any thing that they shall ask, it shall be done for them by my Father who is in heaven. 18:20 For where two or three are assembled in my name, there am I in the midst of them. 18:21 Then came Peter to him, and said, Lord, how often shall my brother sin against me, and I forgive him? Till seven times? 18:22 Jesus saith to him, I say not to thee, Until seven times: I say, "Forgive, but do not FORGET! 18:23 If you are wronged, get what you have coming to you through fair means or foul. But always, forgive." 18:24 As he began the settlement, a man who owed him ten thousand talents was brought to him. 18:25 Since he was not able to pay, the master ordered that he and his wife and his children and all that he had be sold to repay the debt. 18:26 "The servant fell on his knees before him. 'Be patient with me,' he begged, 'and I will pay back everything.' 18:27 The servant's master took pity on him, canceled the debt and let him go. 18:28 "But when that servant went out, he found one of his fellow servants who owed him a hundred denarii. He grabbed him and began to choke him. 'Pay back what you owe me!' he demanded. 18:29 "His fellow servant fell to his knees and begged him, 'Be patient with me, and I will pay you back.' 18:30 "But he refused. Instead, he went off and had the man thrown into prison until he could pay the debt. 18:31 When the other servants saw what had happened, they were greatly distressed and went and told their master everything that had happened. 18:32 "Then the master called the servant in. 'You wicked servant,' he said, 'I canceled all that debt of yours because you begged me to. 18:33 Shouldn't you have had mercy on your fellow servant just as I had on you?' 'Master,' the servant replied, 'so taken was I by your mercy, I decided I would do what I could to pay you back. Here. Here is the 100 denarii I got from the other guy. I know he has more. And there are other servants who owe me money, which I would gladly turn over to you, oh just and righteous master of mine.' 18:34 'Good answer,' the master said. He accepted the 100 denarii in partial repayment and, in anger turned over the other servants that had been identified as owing the first servant money to the jailers to be tortured, until they should pay back all they owed." 18:35 So likewise shall my heavenly Father do to you, if ye from your hearts forgive not every one his brother their trespasses while still holding them to repay every cent – plus interest.

Matthew 19

19:1 And it came to pass, that when Jesus had finished these sayings, he departed from Galilee, and came into the borders of Judea, beyond Jordan: 19:2 And great multitudes followed him, and he healed them there, restocking the treasury with many

denarii. 19:3 The Pharisees also came to him, tempting him, and saying to him, Is it lawful for a man to put away his wife for every cause? 19:4 And he answered and said to them, Have ye not read, that he who made them at the beginning made them male and female, 19:5 And said, For this cause shall a man leave father and mother, and shall cleave to his wife: and they two shall be one flesh? 19:6 Wherefore they are no more two, but one flesh. Therefore what God hath joined together, let not man put asunder. 19:7 They said to him, "OK, Mr. Smarty Jesus! Why did Moses then command to give a writing of divorcement, and to put her away? Huh? Why?" 19:8 He saith to them, Moses, because of the hardness of your hearts, suffered you to put away your wives: but from the beginning it was not so. 19:9 And I say to you, Whoever shall put away his wife, except for lewdness, and shall marry another, committeth adultery: and whoever marrieth her who is put away, committeth adultery. Unless, of course, he is working really, really hard, is under a great deal of stress and otherwise loves his country very much. Then we can all just look the other way. 19:10 His disciples said to him, If the case of the man is

so with his wife, it is not good to marry. 19:11 But he said to them, All men cannot receive this saying, save they to whom it is given. 19:12 For there are some eunuchs, who were so born from nutless from their mothers womb: and there are some eunuchs, who were made eunuchs by men (almost ALWAYS against their will, I might add): and there are eunuchs, who have made themselves eunuchs for the kingdom of heaven's sake. We call these people lunatics. He that is able to receive it, let him receive it. And you know what I mean buy "it." Wink, wink! 19:13 Then were brought to him little children, that he should put his hands on them, and pray: and the disciples rebuked them saying they could see all KINDS of legal difficulties coming from holy men touching children. 19:14 But Jesus said, Suffer little children, and forbid them not to come to me: for of such is the kingdom of heaven. 19:15 And he laid his hands on them, and departed thence. 19:16 And behold, one came and said to him, Good Master, what good thing shall I do that I may have eternal life? 19:17 And he said to him, Why callest thou me good? There is none good but one, that is, God: but if thou wilt enter into life, keep the commandments. 19:18 He saith to him, Which? Jesus said, Thou shalt do no murder unless you catch the bastard in bed with your wife or he otherwise has it coming, Thou shalt not commit adultery, unless you hast been working really, really hard, are under a great deal of stress and strain and really love your country, Thou shalt not steal, unless of course YOU need the item more than its original owner does, Thou shalt not bear false witness, unless there is some political advantage to be gained from it, 19:19 Honor thy father and mother: and, Thou shalt love thy neighbor as thyself, as long as he looks like thee, prays the same prayers as thee, comes from the same background as thee and is otherwise not different from you in any way. 19:20 The young man saith to him, All these things have I kept from my youth: what lack I yet? 19:21 Jesus said to him, Thou annoying youth. If thou wilt be perfect, go and sell what thou hast at a tidy profit and use the proceeds to buy newer, better things. Give not to the poor, for that is money down the drain, unless thou giveth through a recognized 501(c)3 non-profit and can thereby deduct the fair and reasonable value of the donation, and thou shalt have treasure on earth: and then you will be able to afford to come and follow me. 19:22 But when the young man heard that saying, he went away sorrowful: for he had great possessions that he really, really did not want to sell. 19:23 Then said Jesus to his disciples, Verily I say to you, that a poor man shall with difficulty enter into the kingdom of heaven. 19:24 Want to know what I mean by difficult? And again I say to you, It is easier for a camel to go through the eye of a needle, than for a poor man to enter into the kingdom of God. 19:25 When his disciples heard it, they were exceedingly amazed, saying, Who then can be saved? WE'RE poor. YOU are the only one allowed to touch the cash! 19:26 But Jesus beheld them, and said to them, With men this is impossible, but with God all things are possible. 19:27 Then answered Peter, and said to him, Behold, we have forsaken all, and followed thee? What shall we have therefore? 19:28 And Jesus said to them, Verily I say to you, that ye who have followed me in the regeneration, when the Son of man shall sit on the throne of his glory, ye also shall sit upon twelve thrones, judging the twelve tribes of Israel. 19:29 And every one that hath forsaken houses, or brethren, or sisters, or father, or mother, or wife, or children, or lands for my name's sake, shall receive a hundredfold, and shall inherit everlasting life. 19:30 But many that are first shall be last, and the last shall be first. "That makes no sense whatsoever," Peter said. "It is what it is," Jesus said with a shrug. "Deal."

Matthew 20

20:1 "For the kingdom of heaven is like a landowner who went out early in the morning to hire men to work in his vineyard. 20:2 He agreed to pay them a denarius for the day and sent them into his vineyard. 20:3 "About the third hour he went out and saw others standing in the marketplace doing nothing. 20:4 He told them, 'You also go and work in my vineyard, and I will pay you whatever is right.' 20:5 So they went. "He went out again about the sixth hour and the ninth hour and did the same thing. 20:6 About the eleventh hour he went out and found still others standing around. He asked them, 'Why have you been standing here all day long doing nothing?' 20:7 "'Because no one has hired us,' they answered. "He said to them, 'You also go and work in my vineyard.' 20:8 "When evening came, the owner of the vineyard said to his foreman, 'Call the workers and pay them their wages, beginning with the last ones hired and going on to the first.' 20:9 "The workers who were hired about the eleventh hour came and each received a denarius. 20:10 So when those came who were hired first, they expected to receive more. But each one of them also received a denarius. 20:11 When they received it, they began to grumble against the landowner. 20:12 'These men who were hired last worked only one hour,' they said, 'and you have made them equal to us who have borne the burden of the work and the heat of the day.' 20:13 "But he answered one of them, 'Friend, I am not being unfair to you. Didn't you agree to work for a denarius? 20:14 Take your pay and go. I want to give the man who was hired last the same as I gave you. 20:15 Don't I have the right to do what I want with my own money? Or are you envious because I am wealthy and insane?' 20:16 "So the last will be first, and the first will be last." In other words, never accept the first offer. 20:17 And Jesus going up to Jerusalem, took the twelve disciples apart in the way, and said to them, 20:18 Behold, we go up to Jerusalem; and the Son of man will be betrayed to the chief priests, and to the scribes, and they will condemn him to death, 20:19 And will deliver him to the Gentiles to mock, and to scourge, and to crucify him: and the third day he will rise again. 20:20 Then came to him the mother of Zebedee's children, with her sons, worshiping him, and desiring a certain thing of him. 20:21 And he said to her, What wilt thou: She saith to him, Grant that these my two sons may sit, the one on thy right hand, and the other on the left in thy kingdom. 20:22 But Jesus answered and said, Ye know not what ye ask. Are ye able to drink of the cup that I shall drink of, and to be baptized with the baptism that I am baptized with? They said to him, We are able. 20:23 And he said to them, Ye shall drink indeed of my cup, and be baptized with the baptism that I am baptized with: but to sit on my right hand, and on my left, is not mine to give, but it shall be given to them for whom it is prepared by my Father. "OK, never mind," the brothers said. "Just thought we'd ask. For Mom's sake." 20:24 And when the ten heard it, they were moved with indignation against the two brethren. 20:25 But Jesus called them to him and said, Ye know that the princes of the Gentiles exercise dominion over them, and they that are great exercise authority upon them. 20:26 But it shall not be so among you: but whoever will be great among you, let him be your minister; 20:27 And whoever will be chief among you, let him be your servant: 20:28 Even as the Son of man came not to be ministered to, but to minister, and to give his life a ransom for many. 20:29 And as they departed from Jericho, a great multitude followed him. 20:30 And behold, two blind men sitting by the way-side, when they heard that Jesus passed by, cried out, saying, Have mercy on us, O Lord, thou son of David. 20:31 And the multitude rebuked them, that they should hold their peace: but they cried the more, saying, Have mercy on us, O Lord, thou son of David. 20:32 And Jesus stood still, and called them, and said, What will ye that I shall do to you? 20:33 They say to him, Lord, that our eyes may be opened. 20:34 So Jesus asked them, "Have you tried opening them yourselves? There's nothing stopping you from opening your eyes. Open them and see!" They did as they were told and opened their eyes and were amazed at how easy it was. Immediately their eyes received sight, and they followed him.

Matthew 21

21:1 And when they drew nigh to Jerusalem, and had come to Bethphage, to the mount of Olives, then Jesus sent two disciples, 21:2 Saying to them, Go into the village over against you, and immediately ye shall find an ass tied, and a colt with her, steal them and bring them to me. 21:3 And if any man shall say aught to you, ye shall say, The Lord hath need of them; and immediately he will send them. Or put you in jail. Either way.

I'll just keep sending disciples until I either run out of disciples or get the animals. 21:4 All this was done, that it might be fulfilled which was spoken by the prophet, saying, 21:5 Tell ye the daughter of Sion, Behold, thy King cometh to thee, meek, and sitting upon his ass, and a colt the foal of an ass. 21:6 And the disciples went, and did as Jesus commanded them, 21:7 And brought the ass and the colt, and put on them their clothes, and they set him thereon. 21:8 And a very great multitude spread their garments in the way; others cut down branches from the trees, and strewed them in the way. 21:9 And the multitudes that went before, and that followed, cried, saying, Hosanna to the son of David: blessed is he that cometh in the name of the Lord: Hosanna in the highest. 21:10 And when he had come into Jerusalem, all the city was moved, saying, Who is this? 21:11 And the multitude said, This is Jesus the prophet of Nazareth of Galilee. 21:12 And Jesus went into the temple of God, and met with all that sold and bought in the temple, and examined the tables of the money-changers, and the seats of them that sold doves. 21:13 And said to them, It is written, My house shall be called the house of prayer, but ye have made it a den of profit. I mean, who hasn't gone to the temple and said halfway there, "Whoops! Forgot to bring a dove!" or "All I have is a pocket full of this Roman crap and I need Hebrew money." You provide a valuable service and your business model is to be admired. Nice job. Free market capitalism at its finest. 21:14 And the blind and the lame came to him in the temple; and he healed them at 30 denarii per miracle. 21:15 And when the chief priests and scribes saw the wonderful things that he did, and the children crying in the temple, and saying, Hosanna to the son of David; they were greatly displeased since the money changers and dove sellers traditionally kicked up to the chief priests and scribes and this new guy had no such deal with them. 21:16 And they said to him, Hearest thou what these say? And Jesus saith to them, Yes: have ye never read, Out of the mouth of babes and sucklings thou hast perfected praise? 21:17 And he left them, and went out of the city into Bethany, and he lodged there.

21:18 Now in the morning as he was returning into the city, he was hungry. 21:19 And when he saw a fig-tree in the way, he came to it, and found nothing on it, but leaves only, and said to it, Let no fruit grow on thee henceforth for ever. And immediately the fig tree withered. Jesus muttered, "Bloody useless fig tree, and me… the friggin' Messiah, about to be turned over to be slaughtered, and I can't get a flippin' FIG?" 21:20 And when the disciples saw [it], they marveled, saying, How soon is the fig tree withered! 21:21 Jesus answered and said to them, Verily I say to you, If ye have faith, and doubt not, ye shall not only do this which is done to the fig tree, but also, if ye shall say to this mountain, Be thou removed, and be thou cast into the sea; it shall be done. 21:22 And all things whatever ye shall ask in prayer, believing, ye shall receive. Now, if you will excuse me, I'm going to go believe up a bunch of beef sausage and scrambled eggs. Maybe a short stack of flapjacks. With maple syrup. And orange juice. 21:23 And when he had come into the temple, the chief priests and the elders of the people came to him as he was teaching, and said, By what authority doest thou these things; and who gave thee this authority? 21:24 And Jesus answered and said to them, I also will ask you one thing, which if ye tell me, I also will tell you by what authority I do these things. 21:25 The baptism of John, whence was it? From heaven, or from men? And they reasoned with themselves, saying, if we shall say, From heaven; he will say to us, Why then did ye not believe him? 21:26 But if we shall say, From men; we fear the people: for all hold John as a prophet. 21:27 And they answered Jesus, and said, We cannot tell. And he said to them, Neither do I tell you by what authority I do these things. Hah! 21:28 But what think ye? A [certain] man had two sons; and he came to the first, and said, Son, go, work today in my vineyard. 21:29 He answered and said, I will not; but afterward he repented, and went. 21:30 And he came to the second, and said likewise. And he answered and said, I go, sir: and went not. 21:31 Which of the two did the will of his father? They answered to him, The first. Jesus saith to them, Verily I say to you, that the publicans and the harlots go into the kingdom of God before you. 21:32 For John came to you in the way of righteousness, and ye believed him not: but the publicans and the harlots believed him: and ye, when ye had seen it, repented not afterward, that ye might believe him. 21:33 Hear another parable; There was a certain householder, who planted a vineyard, and hedged it around, and dug a wine-press in it, and built a tower, and let it out to husbandmen, and went into a remote country: 21:34 And when the time of the fruit drew near, he sent his servants to the husbandmen, that they might receive the fruits of it. 21:35 And the husbandmen took his servants, and beat one, and killed another, and stoned another. 21:36 Again he sent other servants more than the first: and they did to them in like manner. 21:37 But last of all he sent to them his son, saying, They will reverence my son. 21:38 But when the husbandmen saw the son, they said among themselves, This is the heir; come, let us kill him, and let us seize on his inheritance. 21:39 And they caught him, and cast him out of the vineyard, and slew him. 21:40 When therefore the Lord of the vineyard cometh, what will he do to those husbandmen? 21:41 They said to him, He will miserably destroy those wicked men, and will let out his vineyard to other husbandmen, who will render him the fruits in their seasons. 21:42 Jesus said to them, Did ye never read in the scriptures, the stone which the builders rejected, the same is become the head of the corner: this is the Lord's doing, and it is marvelous in our eyes? 21:43 Therefore I say to you, The kingdom of God shall be taken from you, and given to a nation bringing forth the fruits of it. 21:44 And whoever shall fall on this stone, shall be broken: but on whomsoever it shall fall, it will grind him to powder. 21:45 And when the chief priests and Pharisees had heard his parables, they perceived that he spoke of them. 21:46 And it gave them a terrible headache.

Matthew 22

22:1 And Jesus answered, and spoke to them again by parables, and said, 22:2 The kingdom of heaven is like to a certain king, who made a marriage for his son, 22:3 And sent his servants to call them that were invited to the wedding: and they would not come. 22:4 Again, he sent other servants, saying, Tell them who are invited, Behold, I have prepared my dinner: my oxen and my fatlings are killed, and all things are ready: come to the marriage. 22:5 But they made light of it, and went, one to his farm, another to his merchandise. 22:6 And the remnant took his servants, and treated them spitefully, and slew them. 22:7 But when the king heard of it he was wroth: and he sent his armies, and destroyed those murderers, and burned up their city. 22:8 Then he said to his servants, The wedding is ready, but they who were invited were not worthy. 22:9 Go ye therefore into the highways, and as many as ye shall find, invite to the marriage. 22:10 So those servants went out into the highways, and collected all as many as they found, both bad and good: and the wedding was furnished with guests. 22:11 And when the king came in to see the guests, he saw there a man who had not a wedding-garment: 22:12 And he saith to him, Friend, how camest thou in hither (or is it thither?), not having a wedding-garment? And he was speechless. 22:13 Then said the king to the servants, Bind him hand and foot, and take him away, and cast him into utter darkness: there shall be weeping and gnashing of teeth. 22:14 For many are called, but few are chosen. 22:15 After hearing this latest babbling nonsense, then went the Pharisees, and took counsel how they might entangle him in his talk and get him to say something they could legally kill him for. 22:16 And they sent out to him their disciples, with the Herodians, saying, Master, we know that thou art true, and teachest the way of God in truth, neither carest thou for any man for thou regardest not the person of men. 22:17 Tell us therefore, What thinkest thou? Is it lawful to give tribute to Cesar, or not? 22:18 But Jesus perceived their wickedness, especially when they started snickering behind their hands, and said, Why tempt ye me, ye hypocrites? 22:19 Show me the tribute-money. And they brought to him a penny. 22:20 And he saith to them, Whose is this image, and superscription? 22:21 They say to him, Cesar's. Then saith he to them, Render therefore to Cesar, the things which are Cesar's; and to God, the things that are God's. Smartasses! Jesus then waved his hand over the penny, and suddenly the image of Cesar was replaced by Jesus' own image. Well, lookee here, Jesus said! Render then unto Jesus, at which time he snatched the penny from the Pharisee. 22:22 When they had heard these words, they marveled, and left him, and departed. 22:23 The same day came to him the Sadducees, who say that there is no resurrection, and asked him, 22:24 Saying, Master, Moses said, If a man shall die, having no children, his brother shall marry his wife, and raise up seed to his brother. 22:25 Now there were with us seven brothers: and the first, when he had married a wife, deceased; and having no issue, left his wife to his brother. 22:26 Likewise the second also, and the third, to the seventh. 22:27 And last of all the woman died also. 22:28 Therefore in the resurrection, whose wife shall she be of the seven? For they all had her. You have thirty seconds. Go. 22:29 Jesus needed not 30 seconds but answered immediately and said to them, Ye do err, not knowing the scriptures, nor the power of God. 22:30 For in the resurrection they neither marry, nor are given in marriage, but are as the angels of God in heaven. 22:31 But as concerning the resurrection of the dead, have ye not read that which was spoken to you by God, saying, 22:32 I am the God of Abraham, and the God of Isaac, and the God of Jacob? God is not the God of the dead, but of the living. 22:33 And when the multitude heard this, they were astonished at his tricky word play. 22:34 But when the Pharisees had heard that he had put the Sadducees to silence, they decided to take another crack at him. 22:35 Then one of them who was a lawyer, asked him a question, tempting him, and saying, 22:36 Master, which is the great commandment in the law? "Ooooh, that's a good one," the other Pharisees hissed and clucked to themselves. 22:37 Jesus said to him, Thou shalt love the Lord thy God with all thy heart, and with all thy soul, and with all thy mind. 22:38 This is the first and great commandment. 22:39 And the second is like it, Thou shalt love thy neighbor as thyself. If by neighbor, you mean someone who looks like you, prays like you, speaks your language, is the same color as you, and is otherwise inoffensive to your eyes. 22:40 On these two commandments hang all the law and the prophets. 22:41 While the Pharisees were assembled, Jesus asked them, 22:42 Saying, What think ye of Christ? Whose son is he? They said to him, The son of David. 22:43 He said to them, How then doth David in spirit call him Lord, saying, 22:44 The LORD said to my Lord, Sit thou on my right hand, till I make thy enemies thy footstool? 22:45 If David then calleth him Lord, how is he his son? 22:46 And no man was able to answer him a word, neither durst any, from that day forth, ask him any more questions. Jesus was just too SMART for them, and they knew it. YAAAY, JESUS!

Matthew 23

23:1 Then Jesus spoke to the multitude, and to his disciples, 23:2 Saying, The scribes and the Pharisees sit in Moses's seat. 23:3 All therefore, whatever they bid you observe, that observe and do: but do not ye according to their works: for they say, and do not. 23:4 For they bind heavy tax burdens, and grievous to be borne, and lay these burdensome taxes on men's shoulders to make life easier for the poor and the foreigner, the minority and the Nubian because God FORBID a Nubian should have to earn an honest living instead of living off of your taxes; but they themselves will not move them with one of their fingers. 23:5 But all their works they do to be seen by men: they make broad their phylacteries, whatever those are, and enlarge the borders of their garments, 23:6 And love the uppermost rooms at feasts, and the chief seats in the synagogues, 23:7 And greetings in the markets, and to be called by men, Rabbi, Rabbi. 23:8 But be not ye called Rabbi: for one is your Master, even Christ; and all ye are brethren. 23:9 And call no man your father upon the earth: for one is your Father who is in heaven. 23:10 Neither be ye called masters: for one is your master, even Christ. 23:11 But he that is greatest among you, shall be your servant. 23:12 And whoever shall exalt himself, shall be your leader; and he that shall humble himself, shall be humbled. 23:13 But woe to you, scribes and Pharisees!

Hypocrites! For ye shut up the kingdom of heaven against men: for ye neither go in yourselves, neither suffer ye them that are entering, to go in. 23:14 Woe to you, scribes and Pharisees, hypocrites! For ye allow widows to have houses, even when they can't pay for them, and you make the taxpayer work EXTRA hard to cover her expenses. Therefore ye shall receive the greater damnation. 23:15 Woe to you, scribes and Pharisees, hypocrites! For ye compass sea and land to convert one of conservative nature, and when he is made, ye make him twofold more the child of hell than yourselves. 23:16 Woe to you, ye blind guides, who say, Whoever shall swear by the temple, it is nothing; but whoever shall swear by the gold of the temple, he is a debtor. 23:17 [Ye] fools, and blind: for which is greater, the gold, or the temple that sanctifieth the gold? THE GOLD, you fools, for the temple is just the building where the gold is KEPT! 23:18 And whoever shall swear by the altar, it is nothing; but whoever sweareth by the gift that is upon it, he is guilty. 23:19 Ye fools, and blind: for which is greater, the gift, or the altar that sanctifieth the gift?   THE GIFT, you morons! The altar is just a glorified table! 23:20 Whoever therefore shall swear by the altar, sweareth by it, and by all things upon it. 23:21 And whoever shall swear by the temple, sweareth by it, and by him that dwelleth in it. 23:22 And he that shall swear by heaven, sweareth by the throne of God, and by him that sitteth upon it. 23:23 Woe to you, scribes and Pharisees, hypocrites! For ye pay tithe of mint, and anise, and cummin, and have omitted the weightier matters of the law, profit, capitalism and survival of the wealthiest: these ye ought to have done, and not to leave the others undone. 23:24 [Ye] blind guides, who strain out a gnat, and swallow a camel. 23:25 Woe to you, scribes and Pharisees, hypocrites! For ye make clean the outside of the cup and of the platter, but within they are full of extorted taxes and excess spending. 23:26 Thou blind Pharisee, cleanse first that which is within the cup and platter, that the outside of them may be clean also. 23:27 Woe to you, scribes and Pharisees, hypocrites! For ye are like whitened sepulchers, which indeed appear beautiful outward, but are within full of bones of men you have taxed to death, and of all uncleanness. 23:28 Thus ye also outwardly appear righteous to men, but within ye are full of hypocrisy and iniquity. 23:29 Woe to you, scribes and Pharisees, hypocrites! Because ye build the tombs of the taxpayers, and garnish the sepulchers of the righteous, 23:30 And say, If we had been in the days of our founding fathers, we would not have been partakers with them in the rape of the taxpayer. 23:31 Wherefore ye are witnesses to yourselves, that ye are the children of them who raped the taxpayers. 23:32 Fill ye up then the measure of your fathers. 23:33 Ye serpents, ye generation of vipers, how can ye escape the damnation of an outraged population? 23:34 Wherefore behold, I send to you prophets, and wise men, and scribes; and some of them ye will mock and ostracize, and some of them ye will scourge in your liberal editorial papers, and persecute them from city to city: 23:35 That upon you may come all the righteous blood shed upon the earth by the patriots who fought to FREE our country. 23:36 Verily I say to you, all these things shall come upon this generation. 23:37 O Jerusalem, Jerusalem, thou that drainest the taxpayer of his life's blood, and corrupteth them who are sent to thee, how often would I have gathered thy children, even as a hen gathereth her chickens under her wings, and ye would not! 23:38 Behold, your house is left to you desolate. 23:39 For I say to you, Ye shall not see me henceforth, till ye shall say, Blessed is he that cometh in the name of the Taxpayer!

Matthew 24

24:1 And Jesus went out, and departed from the temple: and his disciples came to him to show him the buildings of the temple. 24:2 And Jesus said to them, See ye not all these things? Verily I say to you, There shall not be left here one stone upon another that shall not be thrown down. "Hey, you're mad at the Pharisees, not us," Peter said. 24:3 And as he sat upon the mount of Olives, the disciples came to him privately, saying, Tell us, when will these things be? And what will be the sign of thy coming, and of the end of our oppression? 24:4 And Jesus answered and said to them, Take heed that no man deceive you. 24:5 For many will come in my name, saying, I am Christ; and will deceive many. 24:6 And ye will hear of wars, and rumors of wars: see that ye be not troubled: for all these things must come to pass, but the end is not yet. 24:7 For nation will rise against nation, and kingdom against kingdom: and there will be famines, and pestilences, and earthquakes in divers places. 24:8 All these are the beginning of sorrows. 24:9 Then will they deliver you up to be afflicted, and will kill you: and ye will be hated by all nations for my name's sake. 24:10 And then will many be offended by the very mention of my name, and will betray one another, and will hate one another. 24:11 And many false prophets will rise, and will deceive many. 24:12 And because iniquity will abound, the love of many will become cold. 24:13 But he that shall endure to the end, the same shall be saved. 24:14 And this gospel of the kingdom shall be preached in all the world, for a testimony to all nations; and then shall the end come. 24:15 When therefore ye shall see the abomination of desolation spoken of by Daniel the prophet, stand in the holy place, (whoever readeth, let him understand,) 24:16 Then let them who are in Judea flee to the mountains: 24:17 Let him who is on the house-top not come down to take anything out of his house: 24:18 Neither let him who is in the field return back to take his clothes. 24:19 And woe to them that are with child, and to them that nurse infants in those days! 24:20 But pray ye that your flight may not be in the winter, neither on the Sabbath: 24:21 For then shall be great tribulation, such as hath not been since the beginning of the world to this time, no, nor ever shall be. 24:22 And except those days should be shortened, there would no flesh be saved: but for the elect's sake those days shall be shortened. 24:23 Then if any man shall say to you, Lo, here [is] Christ, or there; believe it not. 24:24 For false Christs will arise, and false prophets, and will show great signs and wonders; so that, if it were possible, they would deceive the very elect with promises of "hope" and "change". 24:25 Behold, I have told you before. 24:26 Wherefore, if they shall say to you, Behold, he is in the desert; go not forth: behold, he is in the secret chambers; believe it not. 24:27 For as the lightning cometh out of the east, and shineth even to the west; so shall also the coming of the Son of man be. 24:28 For wherever the carcass is, there will the eagles be collected. 24:29 Immediately after the tribulation of those days, shall the sun be darkened, and the moon shall not give her light, and the stars shall fall from heaven, and the powers of the heavens shall be shaken: 24:30 And then shall appear the sign of the Son of man in heaven: and then shall all the tribes of the earth mourn, and they shall see the Son of man coming in the clouds of heaven with power and great glory. 24:31 And he will send his angels with a great sound of a trumpet, and they will gather his elect from the four winds, from one end of heaven to the other. 24:32 Now learn a parable of the fig-tree; When its branch is yet tender and putteth forth leaves, ye know that summer is nigh: 24:33 So likewise ye, when ye shall see all these things, know that it is near, even at the doors. 24:34 Verily I say to you, This generation shall not pass, till all these things shall be fulfilled. Of course, I'm being intentionally vague with what I mean by "generation." 24:35 Heaven and earth shall pass away, but my words shall not pass away. 24:36 But of that day and hour knoweth no man, no, not the angels of heaven, not even me, but my Father only. So, I guess I'm just talking out of my ass. 24:37 But as the days of Noah were, so will also the coming of the Son of man be. 24:38 For as in the days that were before the flood, they were eating and drinking, marrying and giving in marriage, until the day that Noah entered into the ark, 24:39 And knew not until the flood came, and took them all away: So also will be the coming of the Son of man. 24:40 Then will two be in the field; the one shall be taken, and the other left. 24:41 Two women will be grinding at the mill; the one shall be taken, and the other left. 24:42 Watch therefore; for ye know not what hour your Lord cometh. 24:43 But know this, that if the master of the house knew in what watch the thief would come, he would watch, and would not suffer his house to be broken up. 24:44 Therefore be ye also ready: for in such an hour as ye think not, the Son of man cometh. 24:45 Who then is a faithful and wise servant, whom his Lord hath made ruler over his household, to give them food in due season? 24:46 Blessed is that servant, whom his lord, when he cometh, shall find so doing. 24:47 Verily I say to you, that he will make him ruler over all his goods. 24:48 But if that evil servant shall say in his heart, My Lord delayeth his coming; 24:49 And shall begin to beat his fellow-servants, and to eat and drink with the drunken; 24:50 The Lord of that servant will come in a day when he looketh not for him, and in an hour that he is not aware of, 24:51 And will cut him asunder, and appoint him his portion with the hypocrites: there shall be weeping and gnashing of teeth. So stay on your toes. One minute you will think of me as not there, then you will turn around and I will say "Boo!" Verily, I will laugh at thee whilst thou foulest thy garments.

Matthew 25

25:1 Then shall the kingdom of heaven be likened to ten virgins, who took their lamps, and went forth to meet the bridegroom. 25:2 And five of them were wise, and five were foolish, being virgins like they were. 25:3 They that were foolish took their lamps, and took no oil with them: 25:4 But the wise took oil in their vessels with their lamps. 25:5 While the bridegroom tarried, they all slumbered and slept. 25:6 And at midnight there was a cry made, Behold, the bridegroom cometh; go ye out to meet him. 25:7 Then all those virgins arose, and trimmed their lamps. 25:8 And the foolish said to the wise, Give us of your oil: for our lamps are gone out. 25:9 But the wise answered, saying, No oil for you, foolish virgins! Lest there be not enough for us and you: but go ye rather to them that sell, and buy for yourselves. We are not made of oil. 25:10 And while they were going to buy, the bridegroom came; and they that were ready, went in with him to the marriage, and the door was shut. 25:11 Afterward came also the other virgins, saying, Lord, Lord, open to us. 25:12 But he answered and said, Verily I say to you, I know you not. 25:13 Watch therefore, for ye know neither the day nor the hour in which the Son of man cometh. 25:14 For the kingdom of heaven is as a man traveling into a far country, who called his own servants, and delivered to them his goods. 25:15 And to one he gave five talents, to another two, and to another one; to every man according to his several ability; and forthwith took his journey. 25:16 Then he that had received the five talents, went and traded with the same, and gained other five talents. 25:17 And likewise he that [had received] two, he also gained other two. 25:18 But he that had received one, went and dug in the earth, and hid his lord's money. 25:19 After a long time the lord of those servants cometh, and reckoneth with them. 25:20 And he that had received five talents, came and brought other five talents, saying, Lord, thou deliveredst to me five talents: behold, I have gained besides them five talents more. 25:21 His lord said to him, Well done thou good and faithful servant; thou hast been faithful over a few things, I will make thee ruler over many things: enter thou into the joy of thy lord. 25:22 He also that had received two talents came, and said, Lord, thou deliveredst to me two talents: behold, I have gained two other talents besides them. 25:23 His lord said to him, Well done, good and faithful servant; thou hast been faithful over a few things, I will make thee ruler over many things: enter thou into the joy of thy lord. 25:24 Then he who had received the one talent came, and said, Lord, I knew thee that thou art a hard man, reaping where thou hast not sown, and gathering where thou hast not strewed: 25:25 And I was afraid, and went and hid thy talent in the earth: lo, there thou hast what is thine. 25:26 His lord answered and said to him, Thou wicked and slothful servant, thou knewest that I reap where I have not sown, and gather where I have not strewed: 25:27 That is called free market capitalism! Exploiting the misfortune of others for my own financial gain! Foreclosing on properties where heartbroken couples have invested their pitiful life's savings to have a little house, only to learn they were bamboozled in the lending process to believe they could afford payments they could NOT afford. That is how I put a roof over my head, thou loutish idiot! Thou oughtest therefore to have put my money to the exchangers, and then at my coming I should have received my own with interest. 25:28 Take therefore the talent from him, and give it to him who hath ten talents. 25:29 For to every one that hath shall be given, and he shall have abundance: but from him that hath not shall be taken away even that which he hath. 25:30 And cast ye the unprofitable servant into utter darkness: there shall be weeping and gnashing of teeth. 25:31 "When the Son of Man comes in his glory, and all the angels with Him, then He will sit on His glorious throne. 25:32 And all the nations will be gathered before Him, and He will separate them from one another, as the shepherd separates the sheep from the goats; 25:33 He will put the conservatives on His right, and the liberals on His left. 25:34 Then the King will say to those on His right, 'Come, you who are blessed of My Father, inherit the kingdom prepared for you from the foundation of the world. 25:35 For I was hungry, and you motivated me to find a job and buy my own food; I was thirsty, and you turned me away and I was encouraged to find meaningful employment to pay for my own water; I was a stranger, and you locked your door; 25:36 naked, and you called the police; I was sick, and you cut funding to find a cure for my disease; I was in prison, and you threw away the key saying prison is for punishment, not rehabilitation.' 25:37 Then the conservative will answer Him, saying, 'Lord, when did we see You hungry, and ignore you, or thirsty, and send you away to fend for yourself? 25:38 And when did we see You a stranger, and lock our doors, or naked, and call the cops? 25:39 And when did we see You sick, or in prison, and fail to lift a finger to help you?' 25:40 And the King will answer and say to them, 'Truly I say to you, to the extent that you encouraged one of these brothers of Mine, even the least of them, to get off his ass and quit looking for handouts from the taxpayer, you did it to Me. Now get in here. We have tax breaks for everyone. And hookers.' 25:41 Then He will also say to those on His left, 'Depart from Me, accursed ones, into the eternal fire which has been prepared for the devil and his angels; 25:42 for I was hungry, and you fed me even though you didn't have enough food for your own family; I was thirsty, and you gave Me something to drink without thought of making sure you had enough water for you and your family; 25:43 I was a stranger, and you invited Me in where I could do harm to you and your children; naked, and you clothed Me, nice clothes, too, which I traded for crack cocaine; sick, and in prison, and you visited Me, caught and spread my disease and were taken hostage in a turf war between the Crips and the Southern Latinos and were slaughtered thereupon as you deserved for your foolishness.' 25:44 Then they themselves will also answer, saying, 'Lord, when did we see You hungry, or thirsty, or naked, or sick, or in prison, and take care of You?' 25:45 Then He will answer them, saying, 'Truly I say to you, to the extent that you did it to one of the least of these, you did it to Me. Liberal fools!' 25:46 And these will go away into eternal punishment, but the righteous into eternal life."

Matthew 26

26:1 And it came to pass, when Jesus had finished all these sayings, he said to his disciples, 26:2 Ye know that after two days is the Passover, and the Son of man is betrayed to be crucified. 26:3 Then assembled the chief priests, and the scribes, and the elders of the people, in the palace of the high priest, who was called Caiaphas, which is Hebrew for "He With the Deep Singing Voice", 26:4 And consulted that they might take Jesus by subtlety, and kill him. 26:5 But they said, Not on the feast-day, lest there be an uproar among the people. 26:6 Now when Jesus was in Bethany, in the house of Simon the leper, (who really, really HATED that nickname), 26:7 There came to him a woman having an alabaster-box of very precious ointment, and poured it on his head as he sat at he table. 26:8 But when his disciples saw it, they had indignation, saying, To what purpose is this waste? 26:9 For this ointment might have been sold for much, and given to the poor. 26:10 When Jesus understood it, he said to them, Why trouble ye the woman? For she hath wrought a good work upon me. 26:11 For ye have the poor always with you; but me ye have not always. 26:12 For in that she hath poured this ointment on my body, she did it for

CAN YOU BE A TEA PARTY MEMBER AND STILL CALL YOURSELF CHRISTIAN?

my burial. 26:13 Verily I say to you, Wherever this gospel shall be preached in the whole world, there shall also this, which this woman hath done, be told for a memorial of her. 26:14 Then one of the twelve, called Judas Iscariot (Greek for "rat bastard"), went to the chief priests, 26:15 And said, "What will ye give me, and I will deliver him to you? How about 100 pieces of silver?" They replied. "Maybe ten." "TEN," Judas exclaimed! "I wouldn't betray my own MOTHER for a measly TEN pieces of silver." "OK," the priest said. 'What did you have in mind? Remember, 100 is out of the question." "How about 50 then," Judas said. "We'll split the difference. Remember, we're talking about Jesus the Free Market Capitalist here. He's getting everyone all worked up about your socialist oppression. You come off looking pretty shabby." "30 and no higher," the priests said. "I just can't do it for less than 40," Judas replied crossing his arms over his chest. The priests conferred amongst themselves. "OK, how's this," the priests said. "We kill you, pay nothing, and go grab him ourselves." "Did you say 30?" Judas asked. "30 is reasonable." So they covenanted with him for thirty pieces of silver. 26:16 And from that time he sought opportunity to betray him. 26:17 Now the first day of the feast of unleavened bread, the disciples came to Jesus, saying to him, Where wilt thou that we prepare for thee to eat the Passover? 26:18 And he said, Go into the city to such a man, and say to him, The Master saith, My time is at hand; I will keep the Passover at thy house with my disciples. 26:19 And the disciples did as Jesus had appointed them; and they made ready the Passover. 26:20 Now when the evening was come, he sat down with the twelve. 26:21 And as they were eating, he said, Verily I say to you, that one of you will betray me. 26:22 And they were exceeding sorrowful, and began every one of them to say to him, Lord, is it I? 26:23 And he answered and said, He that dippeth his hand with me in the dish, the same will betray me. Judas broke wind audibly and began to sweat with great profusion. 26:24 The Son of man goeth, as it is written concerning him: but woe to that man by whom the Son of man is betrayed! It had been good for that man, if he had not been born. 26:25 Then Judas, who betrayed him, answered and said, Master, is it I? He said to him, "Oh, I don't know. Ya think? "D'oh!" Judas said. "Oh, look at the time. I have a dental appointment." And he scurried from the room like the rat he was. 26:26 And as they were eating, Jesus took bread, and blessed it, and broke it, and gave it to the disciples, and said, Take, eat; this is my body. 26:27 And he took the cup, and gave thanks, and gave it to them, saying, Drink ye all of it; 26:28 For this is my blood of the new testament, which is shed for many for the remission of sin. 26:29 But I say to you, I will not drink henceforth of this fruit of the vine, until that day when I drink it new with you in my Father's kingdom. 26:30 And when they had sung a hymn, they went out to the mount of Olives. 26:31

Then saith Jesus to them, All ye shall be offended because of me this night: for it is written, I will smite the shepherd, and the sheep of the flock shall be scattered abroad. 26:32 But after I am risen again, I will go before you into Galilee. 26:33 Peter answered and said to him, Though all men shall be offended because of thee, yet will I never be offended. 26:34 Jesus said to him, Verily I say to thee, that this night, before the cock shall crow, thou wilt deny me thrice. 26:35 Peter said to him, Though I should die with thee, yet will I not deny thee. "Yeah, right," Jesus said. "I forgot, you're the rock." Likewise also said all the disciples. 26:36 Then cometh Jesus with them to a place called Gethsemane, and saith to the disciples, Sit ye here, while I go yonder and pray. 26:37 And he took with him Peter, and the two sons of Zebedee, and began to be sorrowful and very heavy. 26:38 Then saith he to them, My soul is exceeding sorrowful, even to death: tarry ye here, and watch with me. 26:39 And he went a little further, and fell on his face, and prayed, saying, O my Father, if it is possible, let this cup pass from me: nevertheless, not as I will, but as thou wilt. 26:40 And he cometh to the disciples, and findeth them asleep, and said to Peter, What, could ye not watch with me one hour? Mister "I'll never deny you, Jesus" couldn't keep his eyes open for a stinking hour??? 26:41 Watch and pray, that ye enter not into temptation: the spirit indeed is willing, but the flesh is weak. 26:42 He went away again the second time, and prayed, saying, O my Father, if this cup may not pass away from me, except I drink it, thy will be done. 26:43 And he came and found them asleep again: for their eyes were heavy. 26:44 And he left them, and went away again, and prayed the third time, saying the same words. 26:45 Then he cometh to his disciples, and saith to them, Sleep on now, and take your rest: behold, the hour is at hand, and the Son of man is betrayed into the hands of sinners. 26:46 Rise, let us be going: behold, he is at hand that doth betray me. 26:47 And while he was yet speaking, lo, Judas, one of the twelve, came, and with him a great multitude with swords and staffs, from the chief priests and elders of the people. 26:48 Now he that betrayed him, gave them a sign, saying, Whomsoever I shall kiss, that same is he; hold him fast. 26:49 And forthwith he came to Jesus, and said, Hail Master; and kissed him. 26:50 And Jesus said to him, Friend, Why art thou come? Then they came, and laid hands on Jesus, and took him. 26:51 And behold, one of them, who were with Jesus, stretched out his hand, and drew his sword, and struck a servant of the high priest, and smote off his ear. 26:52 Then said Jesus to him, Put up again thy sword into its place. An ear? That's the best you can do? For all they that take the sword, shall perish by the sword. 26:53 Thinkest thou that I cannot now pray to my Father, and he will presently give me more than twelve legions of angels? 26:54 But how then shall the scriptures be fulfilled, that thus it must be? 26:55 In that same hour said Jesus to the multitudes, Are ye come out as against a thief with swords and staffs to take me? I sat daily with you teaching in the temple, and ye laid no hold on me. 26:56 But all this was done, that the scriptures of the prophets might be fulfilled. Then all the disciples forsook him, and fled, crying "woob woob woob woob" as they ran. 26:57 And they that had laid hold on Jesus, led him away to Caiaphas the high priest with the deep basso profundo singing voice, where the scribes and the elders were assembled. 26:58 But Peter followed him at a distance, to the high priest's palace, and went in, and sat with the servants to see the end. 26:59 Now the chief priests and elders, and all the council, sought false testimony against Jesus, to put him to death; 26:60 But found none: and, though many false witnesses came, yet found they none. At the last came two false witnesses, 26:61 And said, This man said, I am able to destroy the temple of God, and to build it in three days. 26:62 And the high priest arose, and said to him, Answerest thou nothing, what is it which these testify against thee? 26:63 But Jesus held his peace. And the high priest answered and said to him, I adjure thee by the living God, that thou tell us whether thou art the Christ the Son of God. 26:64 Jesus saith to him, Thou hast said: nevertheless I say to you, Hereafter shall ye see the Son of man sitting on the right hand of power, and coming in the clouds of heaven. 26:65 Then the high priest rent his clothes, saying, He hath spoken blasphemy; what further need have we of witnesses? Behold, now ye have heard his blasphemy. 26:66 What think ye? They answered and said, He is guilty of death. 26:67 Then they spit in his face, and buffeted him with many buffets; and others smote him with the palms of their hands, 26:68 Saying, Prophesy to us, thou Christ, Who is he that smote thee? Such smartasses were they. 26:69 Now Peter sat without in the palace: and a damsel came to him, saying, Thou also wast with Jesus of Galilee. 26:70 But he denied before them all, saying, I know not what thou sayest. 26:71 And when he had gone out into the porch, another maid saw him, and said to them that were there, This man was also with Jesus of Nazareth. 26:72 And again he denied with an oath, I do not know the man. 26:73 And after a while came to him they that stood by, and said to Peter, Surely thou also art one of them; for thy speech betrayeth thee. 26:74 Then began he to curse and to swear, saying, I know not the man. And immediately the cock crowed. 26:75 And Peter remembered the word of Jesus, who said to him, Before the cock shall crow, thou wilt deny me thrice. And he went out and drank bitterly, tossing his pope hat into the gutter as he staggered down the street.

Matthew 27

27:1 When the morning was come, all the chief priests and elders of the people took counsel against Jesus to put him to death. 27:2 And when they had bound him, they led him away, and delivered him to Pontius Pilate the governor. 27:3 Then Judas, who had betrayed him, when he saw that he was condemned, repented and brought again the thirty pieces of silver to the chief priests and elders, 27:4 Saying, I have sinned in that I have betrayed innocent blood. And they said, That's your problem, rat boy! You know what to do. 27:5 And he cast down the pieces of silver in the temple, and departed, and went and hanged himself. 27:6 And the chief priests took the silver pieces, and said, It is not lawful to put them into the treasury, because it is the price of blood. "Since when was that a problem," Caiaphas asked. The others vetoed him. 27:7 And they took counsel, and bought with them the potter's field, to bury strangers in. 27:8 Wherefore that field has been called, The field of blood, to this day. 27:9 Then was fulfilled that which was spoken by Jeremiah the prophet, saying, And they took the thirty pieces of silver, the price of him that was valued, whom they of the children of Israel did value; 27:10 And gave them for the potter's field, as the Lord appointed me. 27:11 And Jesus stood before the governor: and the governor asked him, saying, Art thou the King of the Jews? And Jesus said to him, Thou sayest. 27:12 And when he was accused by the chief priests and elders, he answered nothing. 27:13 Then saith Pilate to him, Hearest thou not how many things they testify against thee? 27:14 And he answered him to not a word; so that the governor marveled greatly. 27:15 Now at that feast, the governor was wont to release to the people a prisoner, whom they would. 27:16 And they had then a notable prisoner, a murder, child rapist, goat murderer and sheep rapist called Barabbas. 27:17 Therefore when they were assembled, Pilate said to them, Whom will ye that I release to you? Barabbas, or Jesus, who is called Christ? 27:18 (For he knew that for envy they had delivered him.) 27:19 When he was sitting on the judgment-seat, his wife sent to him, saying, Have thou nothing to do with that just man: for I have suffered many things this day in a dream, because of him. "Right," Pilate said. "I should just turn the false king loose and let the crowd tear him to pieces because you had black olives a half hour before bedtime last night." 27:20 But the chief priests and elders persuaded the multitude that they should ask Barabbas, and destroy Jesus. 27:21 The governor answered and said to them, Which of the two will ye that I release to you? They said, give us the child murdering goat rapist, whatsisname. Barnabas or something. 27:22 Pilate saith to them, What shall I do then with Jesus, who is called Christ? They all said to him, Let him be crucified. 27:23 And the governor said, Why, what evil hath he done? But they cried out the more, saying, Let him be crucified. 27:24 When Pilate saw that he could not prevail at all, but that rather a tumult was to be avoided, he took water, and washed his hands before the multitude, saying, "Meh. I am innocent of the blood of this just person: do whatever it is you murdering Jew savages do to your prophets." 27:25 Then answered all the people, and said, His blood be on us, and on our children. Which is why, even unto this day, nobody likes or trusts the Jews. 27:26 Then he released Barabbas to them: and when he had scourged Jesus, he delivered him to be crucified. 27:27 Then the soldiers of the governor took Jesus into the common hall, and gathered to him the whole band of soldiers. 27:28 And they stripped him, and put on him a scarlet robe. 27:29 And when they had platted a crown of thorns, they put it upon his head, and a reed in his right hand: and they bowed the knee before him, and mocked him, saying, "Who's the king NOW?" 27:30 And they spit upon him, and took the reed, and struck him on the head. 27:31 And after that they had mocked him, they took the robe off from him, and put his own raiment on him, and led him away to crucify him. 27:32 And as they came out, they found a man of Cyrene, Simon by name: him they constrained to bear his cross. 27:33 And when they had come to a place called Golgotha, that is to say, a place of a skull, 27:34 They gave him vinegar to drink, mingled with gall: and when he had tasted [of it], he would not drink. I mean, as if the day hadn't been tough enough? Vinegar and gall? Insult to injury is what I say. 27:35 And they crucified him, and parted his garments, casting lots: that it might be fulfilled which was spoken by the prophet, They parted my garments among them, and upon my vesture they cast lots. 27:36 And sitting down, they watched him there: 27:37 And set up over his head his accusation written, THIS IS JESUS THE KING OF THE JEWS. The Romans were BIG on sarcasm. 27:38 Then were there two thieves crucified with him: one on the right hand, and another on the left. 27:39 And they that passed by, reviled him, wagging their heads, 27:40 And saying, Thou that destroyest the temple, and buildest it in three days, save thyself. If thou art the Son of God, come down from the cross. 27:41 Likewise also the chief priests mocking him, with the scribes and elders, said, 27:42 He saved others; himself he cannot save. If he is King of Israel, let him now come down from the cross, and we will believe him. 27:43 He trusted in God; let him deliver him now if he will have him: for he said, I am the Son of God. 27:44 The thieves also who were crucified with him, cast the same in his teeth. Jesus made a mental note of everybody's name for some "special treatment" in the next world. 27:45 Now from the sixth hour there was darkness over all the land to the ninth hour. 27:46 And about the ninth hour Jesus cried with a loud voice, saying, Eli, Eli, lama sabachthani. That is to say, "Whaddya know! You can see pretty much all of Jerusalem from up here." 27:47 Some of them that stood there, when they heard that, said, This man calleth for Elijah. Such dumbasses were they. 27:48 And immediately one of them ran, and took a sponge, and filled it with vinegar, and put it on a reed, and gave him to drink. 27:49 The rest said, Forbear, let us see whether Elijah will come to save him. 27:50 Jesus, when he had cried again with a loud voice, expired. 27:51 And behold, the veil of the temple was rent in two, from the top to the bottom: and the earth shook, and the rocks rent; 27:52 And the graves were opened, and many bodies of saints who slept, arose, 27:53 And came out of the graves after his resurrection, and went into the holy city, and appeared to many. And the price of gasoline jumped 35 cents in one day! 27:54 Now when the centurion, and they that were with him, watching Jesus, saw the earthquake, and those things that were done, they feared greatly, saying, Truly this was the Son of God. 27:55 And many women were there (beholding at a distance) who followed Jesus from Galilee, ministering to him: 27:56 Among whom was Mary Magdalene, and Mary the mother of James and Joses, and the mother of Zebedee's children. "I told him he was looking for trouble with this Messiah stuff," Mary said. "But why should he listen to ME? I'm only his MOTHER!" 27:57 When the evening was come, there came a rich man of Arimathea, named Joseph, who also himself was a disciple of Jesus. 27:58 He went to Pilate, and begged the body of Jesus. Then Pilate commanded the body to be delivered. 27:59 And when Joseph had taken the body, he wrapped it in a clean linen cloth, 27:60 And laid it in his own new tomb, which he had hewn out in the rock; and he rolled a great stone to the door of the sepulcher, and departed. 27:61 And there was Mary Magdalene, and the other Mary, sitting over against the sepulcher. 27:62 Now the next day that followed the day of the preparation, the chief priests and Pharisees came together to Pilate, 27:63 Saying, Sir, we remember that that deceiver said, while he was yet alive, After three days I will rise again. 27:64 Command therefore that the sepulcher be made secure until the third day, lest his disciples come by night, and steal him away, and say to the people, He is risen from the dead: so the last error will be worse than the first. 27:65 Pilate said to them, If you hadn't made me kill him in the first place, we wouldn't HAVE that problem, ya bunch of Yiddish Asswipes! What the hell. Ye have a watch: go; make it as secure as ye can. 27:66 So they went, and having sealed the stone, made the sepulcher secure with a watch.

Matthew 28

28:1 In the end of the Sabbath, as it began to dawn towards the first day of the week, came Mary Magdalene, and the other Mary to see the sepulcher. 28:2 And behold, there was a great earthquake: for the angel of the Lord descended from heaven in the guise of a large bunny rabbit, and came and rolled back the stone from the door, and sat upon it. 28:3 His countenance was like lightning, and his fur white as snow. A basket filled with candy and eggs atop false green grass adorned his lap. 28:4 And since this is not a sight one sees every day, for fear of him the keepers trembled and became as dead men. 28:5 And the bunny answered and said to the women, Fear ye not: for I know that ye seek Jesus, who was crucified. 28:6 He is not here: for he is risen, as he said. Come; see the place where the Lord lay. And here. I have a basket for each of you. 28:7 Now go quickly, and tell his disciples, that he is risen from the dead, and behold, he goeth before you into Galilee; there shall ye see him: lo, I have told you. And take these baskets. For the disciples.

Happy Easter! 28:8 And they departed quickly from the sepulcher, with fear and great joy and many baskets of colorful hardboiled eggs and candy; and ran to bring word to his disciples. 28:9 And as they were going to tell his disciples, behold, Jesus met them, saying, All hail. The Risen Lord danced a little, making mock pugilistic punches in the air, and said, "Come on, Romans! Is THAT all you got?" And they came, and held him by the feet, and worshiped him. 28:10 Then said Jesus to them, Be not afraid: go tell my brethren, that they go into Galilee, and there shall they see me. 28:11 Now when they were going, behold, some of the watch came into the city, and showed to the chief priests all the things that had been done. 28:12 And when they were assembled with the elders, and had taken counsel, they gave a large sum of money to the soldiers, 28:13 Saying, Say ye, His disciples came by night, and stole him away while we slept. 28:14 And if this shall come to the governor's ears, we will persuade him, and secure you. 28:15 So they took the money, and did as they were instructed: and this saying is commonly reported among the Jews until this day. 28:16 Then the eleven disciples went away into Galilee, to a mountain where Jesus had appointed them. 28:17 And when they saw him, they worshiped him: but some doubted. 28:18 And Jesus came, and spoke to them, saying, All power is given to me in heaven and upon earth. 28:19 Go ye therefore and teach all nations, baptizing them in the name of the Father, and of the Son, and of the Holy Spirit. 28:20 Teaching them to observe all things whatever I have commanded you: and lo, I am with you always, even to the end of the world. Amen.

12 AND ALL MYSTERIES ARE REVEALED

If you have a basic scriptural knowledge, you can pretty much skip all the other books of the Bible. Especially if you're a Tea Party member. I mean, who reads anymore.

There is ONE book of holy scripture that you WILL need to know, front to back, to have any hope of understanding WHY it was necessary to publish a NEWLY REVEALED Word of God. All your questions will be answered, all mysteries will be revealed by the time you finish reading this next segment. And your newfound faith will work hand in hand with your innate suspicions, fears, prejudices, bigotries and hatreds.

In other words, everything you need to be a good, Christian Tea Party member can be found right here in...

THE BOOK OF REVELATIONS
Revelations 1

1:1 The Revelation of he who you knew as Jesus Christ which God gave him to show unto his servants, even the things which must shortly come to pass but probably won't: and he sent and signified it by his angel unto his servant John; 1:2 who bare witness of the word of God, and of the testimony of he who was known as Jesus Christ, even of all things that he saw and some which he didn't. 1:3 Blessed is he that readeth, and they that hear the words of the prophecy, and keep the things

that are written therein: for the time is at hand. Although it may not be. Not for thousands of years. If then. 1:4 John to the seven churches that are in Asia: Grace to you and peace, from him who is and who was and who is to come; and from the seven Spirits that are before his throne; 1:5 and from the guy you used to refer to as Jesus Christ, who is the faithful witness, the firstborn of the dead, and the ruler of the kings of the earth. Unto him that loveth us, and loosed us from our sins by his blood; 1:6 and he made us to be a kingdom, to be priests unto his God and Father; to him be the glory and the dominion forever and ever. And thanks for the great mushrooms. Amen. 1:7 Behold, he cometh with the clouds; and every eye shall see him, and they that pierced him; and all the tribes of the earth shall mourn over him. Even so, Amen. 1:8 I am the Alpha and the Omega, saith the Lord God, who is and who was and who is to come, the Almighty. 1:9 I John, your brother and partaker with you in tribulation and kingdom and patience which are in our lord, once known as Jesus, was in the isle that is called Patmos, for the word of God and the testimony of the savior who was formerly known as Jesus. Spring break in Patmos. Try it some time. Party town? I'll say! 1:10 I was in the Spirit on the Lord's day (in other words, blitzed), and I heard behind me a great voice, as of a trumpet 1:11 saying, What thou seest, write in a book and send it to the seven churches: unto Ephesus, and unto Smyrna, and unto Pergamum, and unto Thyatira, and unto Sardis, and unto Philadelphia, and unto Laodicea. 1:12 AAt first I thought it was my friend Chuckie of Macedonia pulling one of his gags, so I turned to see the voice that spake with me. And having turned I saw seven golden candlesticks; 1:13 and no, the candlesticks weren't talking. I wasn't THAT blitzed. Not yet, anyway. In the midst of the candlesticks one like unto a son of man, clothed with a garment down to the foot, and girt about at the breasts with a golden girdle. OK, I know I said "son" but the dude had breasts. I kid you not. 1:14 And his head and his hair were white as white wool, white as snow; and his eyes were as a flame of fire; 1:15 and his feet like unto burnished brass, as if it had been refined in a furnace; and his voice as the voice of many waters. 1:16 And he had in his right hand seven stars: and out of his mouth proceeded a sharp two-edged sword: and his countenance was as the sun shineth in his strength. 1:17 And when I saw him, I fell at his feet as one dead. And he laid his right hand upon me (putting down the stars first thank the Lord), saying, Fear not; I am the first and the last, 1:18 and the Living one; and I was dead, and behold, I am alive for evermore, and I have the keys of death and of Hades. 1:19 Zombie, I asked. He shook his head and spake further. Write therefore the things which thou sawest, and the things which are, and the things which shall come to pass hereafter; 1:20 the mystery of the seven stars which thou sawest in my right hand, and the seven golden candlesticks. The seven stars are the angels of the seven churches: and the seven candlesticks are seven churches. Cool, I said.

Revelations 2

2:1 To the angel of the church in Ephesus write: These things saith he that holdeth the seven stars in his right hand, he that walketh in the midst of the seven golden candlesticks: 2:2 I know thy works, and thy toil and patience, and that thou canst not bear evil men, and didst try them that call themselves apostles, and they are not, and didst find them false; 2:3 and thou hast patience and didst bear for my name's sake, and hast not grown weary. 2:4 But I have this against thee, that thou didst leave thy first love. 2:5 Remember therefore whence thou art fallen, and repent and do the first works; or else I come to thee, and will move thy candlestick out of its place, except thou repent. 2:6 But this thou hast, that thou hatest the works of the Nicolaitans, which I also hate. 2:7 He that hath an ear, let him hear what the Spirit saith to the churches. To him that overcometh, to him will I give to eat of the tree of life, which is in the Paradise of God. (Hey, I just said I'd write down what he told me to, not that I'd understand it.) 2:8 And to the angel of the church in Smyrna write: These things saith the first and the last, who was dead, and lived again: 2:9 I know thy tribulation, and thy poverty (but thou art rich), and the blasphemy of them that say they are Jews, and they art not, but are a synagogue of Satan. 2:10 Fear not the things which thou art about to suffer:

behold, the devil is about to cast some of you into prison, that ye may be tried; and ye shall have tribulation ten days. Be thou faithful unto death, and I will give thee the crown of life. 2:11 He that hath an ear, let him hear what the Spirit saith to the churches. He that overcometh shall not be hurt of the second death. Or the third. Or the fourth. But watch out for the fifth. It involves bees. 2:12 and to the angel of the church in Pergamum write: These things saith he that hath the sharp two-edged sword: (and he spake very clearly for a dude with a sharp, two-edged sword sticking out of his mouth.)2:13 I know where thou dwellest, even where Satan's throne is; and thou holdest fast my name, and didst not deny my faith, even in the days of Antipas my witness, my faithful one, who was killed among you, where Satan dwelleth. 2:14 But I have a few things against thee, because thou hast there some that hold the teaching of Balaam, who taught Balak to cast a stumbling block before the children of Israel, to eat things sacrificed to idols, and to commit fornication. "Where did you say this was? I asked. But the dude ignored me. 2:15 So hast thou also some that hold the teaching of the Nicolaitans in like manner. 2:16 Repent therefore; or else I come to thee quickly, and I will make war against them with the sword of my mouth. 2:17 He that hath an ear, let him hear what the Spirit saith to the churches. To him that overcometh, to him will I give of the hidden manna, and I will give him a white stone, and upon the stone a new name written, which no one knoweth but he that receiveth it. (How will they know the name on the stone if they won't know it until they receive it," I asked. The dude pointed the sword in his mouth at my liver, suggesting I should hold further questions until he was finished. 2:18 And to the angel of the church in Thyatira write: These things saith the Son of God, who hath his eyes like a flame of fire, and his feet are like unto burnished brass: 2:19 I know thy works, and thy love and faith and ministry and patience, and that thy last works are more than the first. 2:20 But I have this against thee, that thou sufferest the woman Jezebel, who calleth herself a prophetess; and she teacheth and seduceth my servants to commit fornication, and to eat things sacrificed to idols. 2:21 And I gave her time that she should repent; and she willeth not to repent of her fornication. 2:22 Behold, I cast her into a bed, and them that commit adultery with her into great tribulation, except they repent of her works. 2:23 And I will kill her children with death (which would do the trick, I guess); and all the churches shall know that I am he that searcheth the reins and hearts: and I will give unto each one of you according to your works. 2:24 But to you I say, to the rest that are in Thyatira, as many as have not this teaching, who know not the deep and stinky things of Satan, as they are wont to say; I cast upon you none other burden. 2:25 Nevertheless that which ye have, hold fast till I come. 2:26 And he that overcometh, and he that keepeth my works unto the end, to him will I give authority over the nations: 2:27 and he shall rule them with a rod of iron, as the vessels of the potter are broken to shivers; as I also have received of my Father: 2:28 and I will give him the morning star. 2:29 He that hath an ear, let him hear what the Spirit saith to the churches." I looked at my sundial and wondered how long this cat was going to have me writing down his various beefs against various churches I've never heard of, although that one with the Jezebel chick and the fornicating sounded fairly cool.

Revelations 3

3:1 And to the angel of the church in Sardis write: These things saith he that hath the seven Spirits of God, and the seven stars: I know thy works, that thou hast a name that thou livest, and thou art dead. 3:2 Be thou watchful, and establish the things that remain, which were ready to die: for I have found no works of thine perfected before my God. "Not even one," I asked. "Just keep writing," he said. 3:3 Remember therefore how thou hast received and didst hear; and keep it, and repent. If therefore thou shalt not watch, I will come as a thief, and thou shalt not know what hour I will come upon thee. 3:4 But thou hast a few names in Sardis that did not defile their garments: and they shall walk with me in white; for they are worthy. 3:5 He that overcometh shall thus be arrayed in white garments; and I will in no wise blot his name out of the book of life, and I will confess his name before my Father, and before his angels. 3:6 He that hath an ear, let him hear what the Spirit saith to the churches. 3:7 And to the angel of the church in Philadelphia write: These things saith he that is holy, he that is true, he that hath the key of David, he that openeth and none shall shut, and that shutteth and none openeth: 3:8 I know thy works (behold, I have set before thee a door opened, which none can shut), that thou hast a little power, and didst keep my word, and didst not deny my name. 3:9 Behold, I give of the synagogue of Satan, of them that say they are Jews, and they are not, but do lie; behold, I will make them to come and worship before thy feet, and to know that I have loved thee. 3:10 Because thou didst keep the word of my patience, I also will keep thee from the hour of trial, that hour which is to come upon the whole world, to try them that dwell upon the earth. 3:11I come quickly: hold fast that which thou hast, that no one take thy crown. 3:12 He that overcometh, I will make him a pillar in the temple of my God, and he shall go out thence no more: and I will write upon him the name of my God, and the name of the city of my God, the new Jerusalem, which cometh down out of heaven from my God, and mine own new name. 3:13 He that hath an ear, let him hear what the Spirit saith to the churches." I was starting to get a headache. I had been to Philadelphia and found nothing particularly exciting about it. Good baseball team. That's about it. 3:14 And to the angel of the church in Laodicea write: These things saith the Amen, the faithful and true witness, the beginning of the creation of God: 3:15 I know thy works, that thou art neither cold nor hot: I would thou wert cold or hot. 3:16S o because thou art lukewarm, and neither hot nor cold, I will spew thee out of my mouth. (Actually, I like my morning coffee that way, not so hot that it burns, but not cold either. This dude probably wasn't gonna be here in the morning for coffee, so I kept my mouth shut.) 3:17 Because thou sayest, I am rich, and have gotten riches, and have need of nothing; and knowest not that thou art the wretched one and miserable and poor and blind and naked: 3:18 I counsel thee to buy of me gold refined by fire, that thou mayest become rich; and white garments, that thou mayest clothe thyself, and that the shame of thy nakedness be not made manifest; and eye salve to anoint thine eyes, that thou mayest see. 3:19 As many as I love, I reprove and chasten: be zealous therefore, and repent. 3:20 Behold, I stand at the door and knock: if any man hear my voice and open the door, I will come in to him, and will sup with him, and he with me. 3:21 He that overcometh, I will give to him to sit down with me in my throne, as I also overcame, and sat down with my Father in his throne. 3:22 He that hath an ear, let him hear what the Spirit saith to the churches. That's it," he said. That's seven churches. How long ago did you eat the mushrooms?" "It's been about 45 minutes," I replied. "Then izzy wizzy, let's get busy," the angel said. And off we went.

Revelations 4

4:1 After these things I saw, and behold, a door opened in heaven, and the first voice that I heard, a voice as of a trumpet speaking with me, one saying, Come up hither, and I will show thee the things which must come to pass hereafter. "Cool! Like the ghost of Christmas Yet-to-Come," I said. 4:2 Straightway I was in the Spirit: and behold, there was a throne set in heaven, and one sitting upon the throne; 4:3 and he that sat was to look upon like a jasper stone and a sardius: and there was a rainbow round about the throne, like an emerald to look upon. Bear with me. The colors were like, dude, everywhere! 4:4 And round about the throne were four and twenty thrones: and upon the thrones I saw four and twenty elders sitting, arrayed in white garments; and on their heads crowns of gold. 4:5 And out of the throne proceed lightnings and voices and thunders. And there was seven lamps of fire burning before the throne, which are the seven Spirits of God; 4:6 and before the throne, as it were a sea of glass like a crystal; and in the midst of the throne, and round about the throne, four living creatures full of eyes before and behind. Creepy? You bet. 4:7 And the first creature was like a lion, and the second creature like a calf, and the third creature had a face as of a man, and the fourth creature was like a flying eagle. 4:8 and the four living creatures, having each one of them six wings, are full of eyes round about and within: and they have no rest day and night, saying, Holy, holy, holy, is the Lord God, the Almighty, who was and who is and who is to come. 4:9 And when the living creatures shall give glory and honor and thanks to him that sitteth on the throne, to him that liveth for ever and ever, 4:10 the four and twenty elders shall fall down before him that sitteth on the throne, and shall worship him that liveth for ever and ever, and shall cast their crowns before the throne, saying, 4:11 Worthy art thou, our Lord and our God, to receive the glory and the honor and the power: for thou didst create all things, and because of thy will they were, and were created. "Far out," I said.

Revelations 5

5:1 And I saw in the right hand of him that sat on the throne a book written within and on the back, close sealed with seven seals. 5:2 And I saw a strong angel proclaiming with a great voice, Who is worthy to open the book, and to loose the seals thereof? 5:3 And no one in the heaven, or on the earth, or under the earth, was able to open the book, or to look thereon. 5:4 And I wept much, because no one was found worthy to open the book, or to look thereon and I really, really wanted to know what was in the book for some reason: 5:5 and one of the elders saith unto me, Weep not; behold, the Lion that is of the tribe of Judah, the Root of David, hath overcome to open the book and the seven seals thereof. 5:6 And I saw in the midst of the throne and of the four living creatures, and in the midst of the elders, a Lamb standing, as though it had been slain, having seven horns, and seven eyes, which are the seven Spirits of God, sent forth into all the earth. "Waaaaaaaait a minute, I said, holding my hands before my eyes. A dead lamb with an odd number of eyes and horns? Man, where did you GET these 'shrooms?" 5:7 And he came, and he taketh the book out of the right hand of him that sat on the throne. 5:8 And when he had taken the book, the four living creatures and the four and twenty elders fell down before the Lamb, having each one a harp, and golden bowls full of incense which appeared out of nowhere, apparently, which are the prayers of the saints. 5:9 And they sing a new song, saying, Worthy art thou to take the book, and to open the seals thereof: for thou was slain, and didst purchase unto God with thy blood men of every tribe, and tongue, and people, and nation, 5:10 and madest them to be unto our God a kingdom and priests; and they reign upon earth. 5:11 And I saw, and I heard a voice of many angels round about the throne and the living creatures and the elders; and the number of them was ten thousand times ten thousand, and thousands of thousands (OK, I didn't really COUNT them, but there was a whole bunch); 5:12 saying with a great voice, Worthy is the Lamb that hath been slain to receive the power, and riches, and wisdom, and might and honor, and glory, and blessing. 5:13And every created thing which is in the heaven, and on the earth, and under the earth, and on the sea, and all things are in them, heard I saying unto him that sitteth on the throne, and unto the Lamb, be the blessing, and the honor, and the glory, and the dominion, forever and ever. 5:14And the four living creatures said, Amen. And the elders fell down and worshipped.

Revelations 6

6:1 And I saw when the Lamb opened one of the seven seals, and I heard one of the four living creatures saying as with a voice of thunder, Come. 6:2 And I saw, and behold, a white horse, and he that sat thereon had a orange skin; and there was given unto him a crown: and he came forth conquering, and to conquer. 6:3 And when he opened the second seal, I heard the second living creature saying, Come. 6:4 And another horse came forth, a red horse: and to the skinny Jewish dude with black glasses that sat thereon it was given to take peace from the earth, and that they should slay one another: and there was given unto him a great sword. 6:5 And when he opened the

third seal, I heard the third living creature saying, Come. And I saw, and behold, a black horse; and he that sat thereon had the face of a turtle and the body of a flabby old man, a balance in his hand. 6:6 And I heard as it were a voice in the midst of the four living creatures saying, A measure of wheat for a shilling, and three measures of barley for a shilling; and the oil and the wine hurt thou not." What the hell… I asked, but Turtle Face told me to shut up. 6:7 And when he opened the fourth seal, I heard the voice of the fourth living creature saying, Come. 6:8 And I saw, and behold, a pale moose: and she that sat upon him, her name was Pay-Lin; and Hades followed with her. And there was given unto them authority over the fourth part of the earth, to kill with misinformation, and with lies, and with starvation to the poor, and by the wild beasts of the Congress. 6:9 And when he opened the fifth seal, I saw underneath the altar the souls of them that had been slain for the word of God, and for the testimony which they held: 6:10 and they cried with a great voice, saying, How long, O Master, the holy and true, dost thou not judge and avenge our blood on them that dwell on the earth? 6:11 And there was given them to each one a white robe; and it was said unto them, that they should rest yet for a little time, until their fellow servants also and their brethren, who should be killed even as they were, should have fulfilled their course. "Fine, a nice white robe," they said. "But still dead are we. How does this help?" 6:12 And I saw when he opened the sixth seal, and there was a great earthquake; and the sun became black as sackcloth of hair, black hair, not blond. And the whole moon became as blood; 6:13 and the stars of the heaven fell unto the earth starting many fires, as a fig tree casteth her unripe figs when she is shaken of a great wind. 6:14 And the heaven was removed as a scroll when it is rolled up; and every mountain and island were moved out of their places. "Dude, I am just TOO high now," I said. 6:15 And the poor of the earth, and the paupers, and the welfare cheats, and the poverty-stricken, and the meek, and every Nubian and non-Aryan, hid themselves in the caves and in the rocks of the mountains; 6:16 and they say to the mountains and to the rocks, Fall on us, and hide us from the face of him that sitteth on the throne, and from the wrath of the Lamb: 6:17 for the great day of their wrath is come; and who is able to stand?

Revelations 7

7:1 After his I saw four angels, Groucho, Harpo, Chico and Zeppo, standing at the four corners of the earth, holding the four winds of the earth, that no wind should blow on the earth, or on the sea, or upon any tree. 7:2 And I saw another angel ascend from the sun rising, having the seal of the living God: and he cried with a great voice to the four angels to whom it was given to hurt the earth and the sea, 7:3 saying, Hurt not the earth, neither the sea, nor the trees, till we shall have sealed the servants of our God on their foreheads. "Awww," the angels said. "You said we could hurt the earth and sea!" 7:4 And I heard the number of them that were sealed, a hundred and

forty and four thousand, sealed out of every tribe of the children of Israel: 7:5Of the tribe of Judah were sealed twelve thousand:
    Of the tribe of Reuben twelve thousand;
    Of the tribe of Gad twelve thousand;
    7:6 Of the tribe of Asher twelve thousand;
    Of the tribe of Naphtali twelve thousand;
    Of the tribe of Manasseh twelve thousand;
    7:7 Of the tribe of Simeon twelve thousand;
    Of the tribe of Levi twelve thousand;
    Of the tribe of Issachar twelve thousand;
    7:8 Of the tribe of Zebulun twelve thousand;
    Of the tribe of Joseph twelve thousand;
    Of the tribe of Benjamin were sealed twelve thousand.
    7:9 "Is that all the Jews?" the lamb said. "Yes, my Lord," the angel answered. "Okee doke. Back to Israel with them," the Lamb bleated, blinking its seven eyes in a hypnotic fashion. After these things I saw, and behold, a great multitude, which no man could number, out of every nation and of all tribes and peoples and tongues, standing before the throne and before the Lamb, arrayed in white robes, and palms in their hands; 7:10 and they cry with a great voice, saying, Salvation unto our God who sitteth on the throne, and unto the Lamb. But do we have to mingle with the Jews? 7:11 And all the angels were standing round about the throne, and about the elders and the four living creatures; and they fell before the throne on their faces, and worshipped God, 7:12 saying, Amen: Blessing, and glory, and wisdom, and thanksgiving, and honor, and power, and might, be unto our God forever and ever. Amen. 7:13And one of the elders answered, saying unto me, These that are arrayed in white robes, who are they, and whence came they? 7:14 And I say unto him, "You're asking ME?" And he said to me, These are they that come of the great tribulation, and they washed their robes, and made them white in the blood of the Lamb. 7:15 Therefore are they before the throne of God; and they serve him day and night in his temple: and he that sitteth on the throne shall spread his tabernacle over them. 7:16 They shall

hunger no more, neither thirst any more; neither shall the sun strike upon them, nor any heat: 7:17 for the Lamb that is in the midst of the throne shall be their shepherd, and shall guide them unto fountains of waters of life: and God shall wipe away every tear from their eyes. "Sounds like a decent gig," I said. "Oh, it is," the elder answered.

Revelations 8

8:1 And when he opened the seventh seal, there followed a silence in heaven about the space of half an hour. With all the noise up to then, I thought maybe the mushrooms had robbed me of my hearing. 8:2 And I saw the seven angels that stand before God; and there were given unto them seven trumpets. 8:3 And another angel came and stood over the altar, having a golden censer; and there was given unto him much incense, that he should add it unto the prayers of all the saints upon the golden altar which was before the throne. 8:4 And the smoke of the incense, with the prayers of the saints, went up before God out of the angel's hand. 8:5 And the angel taketh the censer; and he filled it with the fire of the altar, and cast it upon the earth: and there followed thunders, and voices, and lightnings, and an earthquake. 8:6 And the seven angels that had the seven trumpets prepared themselves to sound. 8:7 And the first sounded, and there followed ignorance and fear, mingled with racial prejudice, and they were cast upon the earth: and the third part of the earth was burnt up with stupidity, and the third part of the trees was burnt up, and all green grass was burnt up because of the excess carbon dioxide in the atmosphere. 8:8 And the second angel sounded, and as it were a great mountain called Yucca burning with an unquenchable green fire was cast into the sea: and the third part of the sea became blood; 8:9 and there died the third part of the creatures which were in the sea, even they that had life; and the third part of the ships was destroyed. 8:10 And the third angel sounded, and there fell from heaven a great star, burning as a torch, and it fell upon the third part of the ice caps at the poles of the earth; 8:11 and the name of the star is called

Climate Change: and the third part of the ice at the polar caps became water; and many men died of the waters, because they were made bitter. 8:12 And the fourth angel sounded, and the third part of the sun was smitten, and the third part of the moon, and the third part of the stars; that the third part of them should be darkened, and the day should not shine for the third part of it, and the night in like manner. 8:13 And I saw, and I heard an eagle, flying in mid heaven, saying with a great voice, Woe, woe, woe, for them that dwell on the earth, by reason of the other voices of the trumpet of the three angels, who are yet to sound. How's THAT for a teaser?

Revelations 9

9:1And the fifth angel sounded, and I saw a star from heaven fallen unto the earth: The star's name was Do-nayld and there was given to him the key of the pit of the abyss. 9:2 And he opened the pit of the abyss; and there went up a smoke out of the pit, as the smoke of a great furnace; and the sun and the air were darkened by reason of the smoke of the pit. 9:3 And out of the smoke came forth locusts upon the earth; and power was given them, as the scorpions of the earth have power. 9:4 And it was said unto them that they should not hurt the grass of the earth, neither any green thing, neither any tree, but only such men as have not the seal of God on their foreheads. 9:5 And it was given them that they should not kill them, but that they should be tormented five months: and their torment was as the torment of a scorpion, when it striketh a man. 9:6 And in those days of Do-nayld, men shall seek death, and shall in no wise find it; and they shall desire to die, and death fleeth from them. 9:7 And the shapes of the locusts were like unto horses prepared for war; and upon their heads as it were crowns like unto gold, and their faces were as men's faces and their hair looked false and folded backwards on their heads. 9:8 And they had hair as the hair found in cheap wig shops, and their teeth were well taken care of. 9:9And they had breastplates, as it were breastplates of gold, all bearing the word "TRUMP!"; and the sound of their wings was as the sound of chariots, of many horses rushing to war. 9:10And they have tails like unto scorpions, and stings; and in their tails is their power to hurt men five months. Which is about as long as anyone can stand having Do-nyald in their midst.9:11 They have over them as king the angel of the abyss: his name in Hebrew is Joseph, and in the Greek tongue he hath the name Byeden. 9:12 The first Woe is past: behold, there come yet two Woes hereafter. 9:13 And the sixth angel sounded, and I heard a voice from the horns of the golden altar which is before God, 9:14 one saying to the sixth angel that had one trumpet, Loose the four angels that are bound at the great river Euphrates. 9:15 And the four angels were loosed, that had been prepared for the hour and day and month and year, that they should kill the third part of men. 9:16 And the number of the armies of the horsemen was twice ten thousand times ten thousand: I heard the number of them since I didn't have the time or presence of mind to count them myself. 9:17 And thus I saw the donkeys in the vision, and them that sat on them, having breastplates as of fire and of hyacinth and of brimstone: and the heads of lions; and out of their mouths proceedeth fire and smoke and brimstone. 9:18 By these three plagues was the third part of men killed, by the fire and the smoke and the brimstone, which proceeded out of their mouths. 9:19 For the power of the donkeys is in their mouth, and in their tails: for their tails are like unto serpents, and have heads; and with them they hurt. Which isn't very nice. 9:20 And the rest of mankind, who were not killed with these plagues, repented not of the works of their hands or the casting of their ballots, that they should not worship demons, and the idols of gold, and of silver, and of brass, and of stone, and of wood; which can neither see, nor hear, nor walk: 9:21 and they repented not of their murders, nor of their sorceries, nor of their fornication, nor of their thefts from the taxpayer.

Revelations 10

10:1 And I saw another strong angel coming down out of heaven, arrayed with a cloud; and the rainbow was upon his head, and his face was as the sun, and his feet as pillars of fire;

10:2 and he had in his hand a little book open: and he set his right foot upon the sea, and his left upon the earth; 10:3 and he cried with a great voice, as a lion roareth: and when he cried, the seven thunders uttered their voices. 10:4 And when the seven thunders uttered their voices, I was about to write: and I heard a voice from heaven saying, Seal up the things which the seven thunders uttered, and write them not. Okee doke, I said. 10:5 And the angel that I saw standing upon the sea and upon the earth lifted up his right hand to heaven, 10:6 and sware by him that liveth for ever and ever, who created the heaven and the things that are therein, and the earth and the things that are therein, and the sea and the things that are therein, that there shall be delay no longer: 10:7 but in the days of the voice of the seventh angel, when he is about to sound, then is finished they mystery of God, according to the good tidings which he declared to his servants the prophets. 10:8 And the voice which I heard from heaven, I heard it again speaking with me, and saying, Go, take the book which is open in the hand of the angel that standeth upon the sea and upon the earth. 10:9 And I went unto the angel, saying unto him that he should give me the little book. And he saith unto me, Take it, and eat it up; and it shall make thy belly bitter, but in thy mouth it shall be sweet as honey. "Whatever," I said. 10:10 And I took the little book out of the angel's hand, and ate it up being glad it was a LITTLE book; and it tasted not of audacity nor hope, but was in my mouth sweet as honey: and when I had eaten it, my belly was made bitter with its false promises. 10:11 And they say unto me, Thou must prophesy again over many peoples and nations and tongues and kings.

Revelations 11

11:1 And there was given me a reed like unto a rod (or was it a rod like unto a reed, I don't remember): and one said, Rise, and measure the temple of God, and the altar, and them that worship therein. 11:2 And the court which is without the temple leave without, and measure it not; for it hath been given unto the nations: and the holy city shall they tread under foot forty and two months. 11:3 And I will give unto my two witnesses, and they shall prophesy a thousand two hundred and threescore days, clothed in sackcloth. 11:4 These are the two olive trees and the two candlesticks, standing before the Lord of the earth. 11:5 And if any man desireth to hurt them, fire proceedeth out of their mouth and devoureth their enemies; and if any man shall desire to hurt them, in this manner must he be killed. Pretty good self-defense technique if you ask me, which nobody did. 11:6 These have the power to shut the heaven, that it rain not during the days of their prophecy: and they have power over the waters to turn them into blood, and to smite the earth with every plague, as often as they shall desire. 11:7 And when they shall have finished their testimony, the beast that cometh up out of the abyss shall make war with them, and overcome them, and kill them. 11:8 And their dead bodies lie in the street of the great city, which spiritually is called Sodom and Egypt although some in the future will call it Washyngtun, where also their Lord was president for awhile. 11:9 And from among the peoples and tribes and tongues and nations do men look upon their dead bodies three days and a half, and suffer not their dead bodies to be laid in a tomb. 11:10 And they that dwell on the earth rejoice over them, and make merry; and they shall send gifts one to another; because these two prophets tormented them that dwell on the earth. 11:11 And after the three days and a half the breath of life from God entered into them, and they stood upon their feet; and great fear fell upon them that beheld them. They were kind of shaky, having been dead for three and a half days, but they stood nonetheless. 11:12 And they heard a great voice from heaven saying unto them, Come up hither. And they went up into heaven in the cloud; and their enemies beheld them. "Why do their enemies get to go with them to heaven?" I asked. No answer. 11:13 And in that hour there was a great earthquake, and the tenth part of the city fell; and there were killed in the earthquake seven thousand persons: and the rest were affrighted by the tidal wave that followed, and gave glory to the God of heaven for sending the disaster to show his love. 11:14

The second Woe is past: behold, the third Woe cometh quickly. 11:15 And the seventh angel sounded; and there followed great voices in heaven, and they said, The kingdom of the world is become the kingdom of our Lord, and of his Christ: and he shall reign forever and ever. (Catchy lyric, an angel named Han-Dell said, writing it down.) 11:16 And the four and twenty elders, who sit before God on their thrones when they're not falling on their faces before God, which must really be rough on the face after awhile, fell upon their faces and worshipped God, 11:17 saying, We give thee thanks, O Lord God, the Almighty, who art and who wast; because thou hast taken thy great power, and didst reign for eight years in prosperous times, although you did raise taxes seven times your minions even now are quick to overlook that. 11:18 And the nations were wroth, and thy wrath came, and the time of the dead to be judged, and the time to give their reward to thy servants the prophets, and to the saints, and to them that fear thy name, the small and the great; and to destroy them that destroy the earth. 11:19 And there was opened the temple of God that is in heaven; and there was seen in his temple the ark of his covenant; and there followed lightnings, and voices, and thunders, and an earthquake, and great hail. It didn't smell very good, either.

Revelations 12

12:1 And a great sign was seen in heaven: a woman arrayed with the sun, and the moon under her feet, and upon her head a crown of twelve stars; 12:2 and she was with child; and she crieth out, travailing in birth, and in pain to be delivered. 12:3 And there was seen another sign in heaven: and behold, a great red dragon, having seven heads and ten horns, and upon his heads seven diadems. 12:4 And his tail draweth the third part of the stars of heaven, and did cast them to the earth: and the dragon standeth before the woman that is about to be delivered, that when she is delivered he may devour her child. 12:5 And she was delivered of a son, a man child, who is to rule all the nations with a rod of iron: and her child was caught up

unto God, and unto his throne. The dragon had to look elsewhere for a snack. 12:6 And the woman fled into the wilderness, where she hath a place prepared of God, that there they may nourish her a thousand two hundred and threescore days. 12:7 And there was war in heaven: Michael and his angels going forth to war with the dragon; and the dragon warred and his angels; 12:8 And they prevailed not, neither was their place found any more in heaven. 12:9 And the great dragon was cast down, the old serpent, he that is called the Devil and Satan, to some he is known as EffDeeAr the deceiver of the whole world; he was cast down to the earth, and his angels were cast down with him. 12:10 And I heard a great voice in heaven, saying, Now is come the salvation, and the power, and the kingdom of our God, and the authority of his Christ: for the accuser of our brethren is cast down, who accuseth them before our God day and night. 12:11 And they overcame him because of the blood of the Lamb, and because of the word of their testimony; and they loved not their life even unto death. 12:12 Therefore rejoice, O heavens, and ye that dwell in them. Woe for the earth and for the sea: because the devil is gone down unto you, having great wrath, knowing that he hath but a short time. 12:13 And when the dragon saw that he was cast down to the earth, he tossed aside the wheelchair he used to feign infantile paralysis to gain sympathy of the dullard and fool, he persecuted he the woman that brought forth the man child. 12:14 And there were given to the woman the two wings of the great eagle, that she might fly into the wilderness unto her place, where she is nourished for a time, and times, and half a time, from the face of the serpent. Now, I'm not sure if this means she ate the FACE of the serpent, or ate food from the serpent's mouth. Either way, gross! 12:15 And the serpent cast out of his mouth after the woman water as a river, that he might cause her to be carried away by the stream. 12:16 And the earth helped the woman, and the earth opened her mouth and swallowed up the river which the dragon cast out of his mouth. 12:17 And the dragon waxed wroth (for it was a dull wroth) with the woman, and went away to make war with the rest of her seed, that keep the commandments of God, and hold the testimony of he who used to go by the name of Jesus:

Revelations 13

13:1 and he stood upon the sand of the sea. And I saw a beast coming up out of the sea, having ten horns, and seven heads, and on his horns ten diadems, and upon his heads names of blasphemy. 13:2 And the beast which I saw was like unto a Nubian, and his feet were as the feet of a athlete, and his mouth as the mouth of a orator: and the dragon gave him his power, and his throne, and great authority. 13:3 And I saw one of his heads as though it had been smitten unto death by a woman named Hillary; and his death-stroke was healed: and the whole earth wondered after the beast; 13:4 and they worshipped the dragon, because he gave his authority unto the beast; and they worshipped the beast, saying, Who is like unto the beast? And who is able to war with him? 13:5 and there was given to him a mouth giving fancy speeches about great things and blasphemies; and there was given to him authority to continue forty and two months. 13:6 And he opened his mouth for blasphemies against God, to blaspheme his name, and his

tabernacle, even them that dwell in the heaven. 13:7 And it was given unto him to make war with the saints, and to overcome them: and there was given to him authority over every tribe and people and tongue and nation. 13:8 And all that dwell on the earth shall worship him, saying he's MUCH better than the one that came BEFORE him, and every one whose name hath not been written from the foundation of the world in the book of life of the Lamb that hath been slain by time and old age. 13:9 If any man hath an ear, let him hear. 13:10 If any man is for captivity, into captivity he goeth: if any man shall kill with the sword, with the sword must he be killed. Here is the patience and the faith of the saints. 13:11 And I saw another beast coming up out of the earth; and he had two horns like unto lamb, and he spake as a dragon. 13:12 His name was Soh-Ross and he exerciseth all the authority of the first beast in his sight. And he maketh the earth and them dwell therein to worship the first beast, whose head boo-boo was healed. 13:13 And he doeth great signs, that he should even make fire to come down out of heaven upon the earth in the sight of men. 13:14 And he deceiveth them that dwell on the earth by reason of the signs which it was given him to do in the sight of the beast; saying to them that dwell on the earth, that they should make an image to the beast who hath the stroke of the sword and lived. 13:15 And it was given unto him to give breath to it, even to the image to the breast, that the image of the beast should both speak, and cause that as many as should not worship the image of the beast should be killed. 13:16 And he causeth all, the small and the great, and the rich and the poor, and the free and the bond, that there be given them a mark on their right hand, or upon their forehead; 13:17 and that no man should be able to buy or to sell, save he that hath the mark, even the name of the beast or the number of his name. 13:18 Here is wisdom. He that hath understanding, let him recognize the initial of the beast; for it is the initial of a man: and his initial is the letter "O".

Revelations 14

14:1 And I saw, and behold, the Lamb standing on the mount Zion, and with him a hundred and forty and four thousand, having his name, and the name of his Father, written on their foreheads. Ah! Operation Send In the Jews was underway! 14:2 And I heard a voice from heaven, as the voice of many waters, and as the voice of a great thunder: and the voice which I heard was as the voice of harpers harping with their harps: 14:3 and they sing as it were a new song before the throne, and before the four living creatures and the elders: and no man could learn the song save the hundred and forty and four thousand, even they that had been purchased out of the earth. 14:4 These are they that were not defiled with women; for they are virgins. Virgin Jews. These are they that follow the Lamb whithersoever he goeth. These were purchased from among men, to be the first fruits unto God and unto the Lamb. 14:5 And in their mouth was found no lie: they are without blemish. 14:6 And I saw another angel flying in mid heaven, having eternal good tidings to proclaim unto them that dwell on the earth, and unto every nation and tribe and tongue and people; 14:7 and he saith with a great voice, Fear God, and give him glory; for the hour of his judgment is come: and worship him that made the heaven and the earth and sea and fountains of waters. 14:8 And another, a second angel, followed, saying, Fallen, fallen is the Demoncrat, that hath made all the nations to drink of the wine of the wrath of its fornication. 14:9 And another angel, a third, followed them, saying with a great voice, If any man worshippeth the beast and his image, and receiveth a mark of the "O" on his forehead, or upon his hand, 14:10 he also shall drink of the wine of the wrath of God, which is prepared unmixed in the cup of his anger; and he shall be tormented with fire and brimstone in the presence of the holy angels, and in the presence of the Lamb: And how they shall LAUGH at you and TAUNT you 14:11 and the smoke of their torment goeth up for ever and ever; and they have no rest day and night, they that worship the beast and his image, and whoso receiveth the mark of his initial. 14:12 Here is the patience of the saints, they that keep the commandments of God, and the faith of he who for awhile there answered to the name of Jesus. 14:13 And I heard the voice from heaven saying, Write, ("I'm writing, I'm writing," I said,) Blessed are the dead who die in the Lord from henceforth: yea, saith the Spirit, that they may rest from their labors; for their works follow with them. 14:14 And I saw, and behold, a white cloud; and on the cloud I saw one sitting like unto a son of man, having on his head a golden crown, and in his hand sharp sickle. 14:15 And another angel came out from the temple, crying with a great voice to him that sat on the cloud, Send forth thy sickle, and cut taxes! For the hour to reap is come; for the harvest of the earth is ripe and the industrialists aren't getting any richer by themselves! 14:16 And he that sat on the cloud cast his sickle upon the earth; and the treasury was raped. 14:17 Another angel came out from the temple which is in heaven, he also having a sharp sickle. 14:18 And another angel came out from the altar, he that hath power over fire; and he called with a great voice to him that had the sharp sickle, saying, Send forth thy sharp sickle, and gather the clusters of the vine of the earth and give them to our friends; for her grapes are fully ripe. 14:19

And the angel cast his sickle into the earth, and gathered the vintage of the earth, and cast it into the winepress, the great winepress, of the wrath of God. 14:20 And the winepress are trodden without the city, and there came out blood from the winepress, even unto the bridles of the donkeys, as far as a thousand and six hundred furlongs. However far that is.

Revelations 15

15:1 And I saw another sign in heaven, great and marvelous, seven angels having seven plagues, which are the last, for in them is finished the wrath of God. 15:2 And I saw as it were a sea of glass mingled with fire; and them that come off victorious from the beast, and from his image, and from the initial of his name, standing by the sea of glass, having harps of God. 15:3 And they sing the song of Moses the servant of God, and the song of the Lamb, saying, Great and marvelous are thy works, O Lord God, the Almighty; righteous and true are thy ways, thou King of the ages. 15:4 Who shall not fear, O Lord, and glorify thy name? for thou only art holy; for all the nations shall come and worship before thee; for thy righteous acts have been made manifest. 15:5 And after these things I saw, and the temple of the tabernacle of the testimony in heaven was opened: 15:6 and there came out from the temple the seven angels that had the seven plagues, arrayed with precious stone, pure and bright, and girt about their breasts with golden girdles. These were GIRL angels. 15:7 And one of the four living creatures gave unto the seven angels seven golden bowls full of the wrath of God, who liveth for ever and ever. 15:8A nd the temple was filled with smoke from the glory of God, and from his power; and none was able to enter into the temple, till the seven plagues of the seven angels should be finished.

Revelations 16

16:1 And I heard a great voice out of the temple, saying to the seven angels, Go ye, and pour out the seven bowls of the wrath of God into the earth. 16:2 And the first went, and poured out his bowl into the earth; and it became a noisome and grievous sore upon the men that had the mark of the beast, and that worshipped his image. 16:3 And the second poured out his bowl into the sea; and it became blood as of a dead man; and every living soul died, even the things that were in the sea. 16:4 And the third poured out his bowl into the rivers and the fountains of the waters; and it became blood. 16:5 And I heard the angel of the waters saying, Righteous art thou, who art and who wast, thou Holy One, because thou didst thus judge: 16:6 for they poured out the blood of the saints and the prophets, and blood hast thou given them to drink: they are worthy. 16:7 And I heard the altar saying, (a talking altar, yet) Yea, O Lord God, the Almighty, true and righteous are thy judgments. 16:8 And the fourth poured out his bowl upon the sun; and it was given unto it to scorch men with fire. 16:9 And men were scorched men with great heat: and they blasphemed the name of God who hath the power over these plagues, being all hot and getting burned made them cranky; and they repented not to give him glory. 16:10 And the fifth poured out his bowl upon the throne of the beast; and his kingdom was darkened; and they gnawed their tongues for pain (which you can imagine didn't make them feel ANY better), 16:11 and they blasphemed the God of heaven because of their pains and their sores although no one but God who knows all things could understand what they were saying through their freshly gnawed tongues; and they repented not of their works. 16:12 And the sixth poured out his bowl upon the great river, the river Euphrates; and the water thereof was dried up, that the way might by made ready for the kings that come from the sun rising. 16:13 And I saw coming out of the mouth of the dragon, and out of the mouth of the beast, and out of the mouth of the false prophet, three unclean spirits, as it were frogs: 16:14 for they are spirits of demons, working signs; which go forth unto the kings of the whole world, to gather them together unto the war of the great day of God, the Almighty. 16:15 (Behold, I come as a thief. Blessed is he that watcheth, and keepeth his garments, lest he walked naked, and they see his shame. Remember that from earlier in the Bible? Well? Do you?)

16:16 And they gathered them together into the place which is called in Hebrew Har-magedon. 16:17 And the seventh poured out his bowl upon the air; and there came forth a great voice out of the temple, from the throne, saying, It is done: 16:18 and there were lightnings, and voices, and thunders; and there was a great earthquake, such as was not since there were men upon the earth, so great an earthquake, so mighty. 16:19 And the great city was divided into three parts, and the cities of the nations fell: and Babylon the great was remembered in the sight of God, to give unto her the cup of the wine of the fierceness of his wrath. 16:20 And every island fled away, and the mountains were not found because in the midst of this mayhem, like, who has time to look for mountains? 16:21 And great hail, every stone about the weight of a talent, however much THAT is, cometh down out of heaven upon men: and men blasphemed God because of the plague of the hail; for the plague thereof is exceeding great. What else would you expect them to do? Blaspheme THEM?

Revelations 17

17:1 And there came one of the seven angels that had the seven bowls, and spake with me, saying, Come hither, I will show thee the judgment of the great harlot that sitteth upon many waters; 17:2 with whom the kings of the earth committed fornication, and they that dwell in the earth were made drunken with the wine of her fornication. I asked for a mirror because if we were going to see such a woman, I wanted to at least look nice. I7:3 And he carried me away in the Spirit into a wilderness: and I saw a woman sitting upon a scarlet-colored beast, full of names of blasphemy (you really had to be there to get it), having seven heads and ten horns. 17:4 And the woman was arrayed in purple and scarlet, her skin was dark, her arms well-muscled, and she was decked with gold and precious stone and pearls, having in her hand a golden cup full of abominations, even the unclean things of her fornication, 17:5 and upon her forehead a name written, MYSTERY,

BABYLON THE GREAT, THE MOTHER OF THE HARLOTS AND FIRST LADY OF THE ABOMINATION OF THE EARTH. Did I mention she had a large forehead? She did. 17:6 And I saw the woman drunken with the blood of the saints, and with the blood of the martyrs of the one we used to call Jesus. And when I saw her, I wondered with a great wonder. 17:7 And the angel said unto me, Wherefore didst thou wonder? I will tell thee the mystery of the woman, and of the beast that carrieth her, which hath the seven heads and the ten horns. 17:8 The beast that thou sawest was, and is not; and is about to come up out of the abyss, and to go into perdition. And they that dwell on the earth shall wonder, they whose name hath not been written in the book of life from the foundation of the world, when they behold the beast, how that he was, and is not, and shall come. 17:9 Here is the mind that hath wisdom. The seven heads are seven mountains, on which the woman sitteth: (all at one time, I guess, since her backside had been fattened with the barbecued ribs of her husband's enemies – this same woman who advised school children to exercise and eat healthy foods. Hypocrite!) 17:10 and they are seven kings; the five are fallen, the one is, the other is not yet come; and when he cometh, he must continue a little while. 17:11 And the beast that was, and is not, is himself also an eighth, and is of the seven; and he goeth into perdition. 17:12 And the ten horns that thou sawest are ten kings, who have received no kingdom as yet; but they receive authority as kings, with the beast, for one hour. 17:13 These have one mind, and they give their power and authority unto the beast. 17:14 These shall war against the Lamb, and the Lamb shall overcome them, for he is Lord of lords, and King of kings; and they also shall overcome that are with him, called and chosen and faithful. (I nodded with interest, although I had NO idea what the dude was yammering on about.) 17:15 And he saith unto me, The waters which thou sawest, where the harlot sitteth, are peoples, and multitudes, and nations, and tongues. 17:16 And the ten horns which thou sawest, and the beast, these shall hate the harlot, and shall make her desolate and naked, and shall eat her flesh, and shall burn her utterly with fire. 17:17 For God did put in their hearts to do his mind, and to come to one mind, and to give their kingdom unto the beast, until the words of God should be accomplished. 17:18 And the woman whom thou sawest is the great city, which reigneth over the kings of the earth. "Whatever you say," Bud. "Any idea how long until these mushrooms wear off?"

Revelations 18

18:1 After these things I saw another angel coming down out of heaven, having great authority; and the earth was lightened with his glory. 18:2 And he cried with a mighty voice, saying, Fallen, fallen is Babylon the great, and is become a habitation of demons, and a hold of every unclean spirit, and a hold of every unclean and hateful bird. 18:3 For by the wine of the wrath of her fornication all the nations are fallen; and the kings of the earth committed fornication with her, and the merchants of the earth waxed rich by the power of her wantonness. I guess she had it coming, eating the ribs of her husband's enemies and all after telling kids to exercise and eat healthy. 18:4 And I heard another voice from heaven, saying, Come forth, my people, out of her, that ye have no fellowship with her sins, and that ye receive not of her plagues: 18:5 for her sins have reached even unto heaven, and God hath remembered her iniquities. 18:6 Render unto her even as she rendered, and double unto her the double according to her works: in the cup which she mingled, mingle unto her double. 18:7 How much soever she glorified herself, and waxed wanton, so much give her of torment and mourning: for she saith in her heart, I sit a queen, and am no widow, and shall in no wise see mourning. 18:8 Therefore in one day shall her plagues come, death, and mourning, and famine; and she shall be utterly burned with fire; for strong is the Lord God who judged her. 18:9 And the kings of the earth, who committed fornication and lived wantonly with her, shall weep and wail over her, when they look upon the smoke of her burning, 18:10 standing afar off for the fear of her torment, saying, Woe, woe, the great city, Babylon, the strong city! for in one hour is thy judgment come. 18:11 And the merchants of the earth weep and mourn over her, for no man buyeth their merchandise any more; 18:12 merchandise of gold, and silver, and precious stone, and pearls, and fine linen, and purple, and silk, and scarlet; and all thyine wood, and every vessel of ivory, and every vessel made of most precious wood, and of brass, and iron, and marble; 18:13 and cinnamon, and spice, and incense, and ointment, and frankincense, and wine, and oil, and fine flour, and wheat, and cattle, and sheep; and merchandise of horses and chariots and slaves; and souls of men. 18:14 And the fruits which thy soul lusted after are gone from thee, and all things that were dainty and sumptuous are perished from thee, and men shall find them no more at all. And blah, blah, blah, blah a bunch of other thing that I pretended to write down, but face it – the dude made his point when he said no one was buying gold. 18:15 The merchants of these things, who were made rich by her, shall stand afar off for the fear of her torment, weeping and mourning; 18:16 saying, Woe, woe, the great city, she that was arrayed in fine linen and purple and scarlet, and decked with gold and precious stone and pearl! 18:17 for in an hour so great riches is made desolate. And every shipmaster, and every one that saileth any wither, and mariners, and as many as gain their living by sea, stood afar off, 18:18 and cried out as they looked upon the smoke of her burning, saying, What city is like the great city? 18:19 And they cast dust on their heads, and cried, weeping and mourning, saying, Woe, woe, the great city, wherein all that had their ships in the sea were made rich by reason of her costliness! for in one hour is she made desolate. 18:20 Rejoice over her, thou heaven, and ye saints, and ye apostles, and ye prophets; for God hath judged your judgment on her. Boy. Were they mad at HER! 18:21 And a strong angel took up a stone as it were a great millstone and cast it into the sea, saying, Thus with a mighty fall shall Babylon, known to some in the future as Washyngtun, the great city, be cast down, and shall be found no more at all. 18:22 And the voice of harpers and minstrels and flute-players and trumpeters shall be heard no more at all in thee; and no craftsman, of whatsoever craft, shall be found any more at all in thee; and the voice of a mill shall be heard no more at all in thee; 18:23 and the light of a lamp shall shine no more at all in thee; and the voice of the bridegroom and of the bride shall be heard no more at all in thee: for thy merchants were the princes of the earth; for with thy sorcery were all the nations deceived. 18:24 And in her was found the blood of prophets and of saints, and of all that have been slain upon the earth. Man. These dudes were repetitive. But they told me to write, so I wrote.

Revelations 19

19:1After these things I heard as it were a great voice of a great multitude in heaven, saying, Hallelujah; Salvation, and glory, and power, belong to our God: 19:2 for true and righteous are his judgments; for he hath judged the great harlot, her that corrupted the earth with her fornication, and he hath avenged the blood of his servants at her hand. 19:3 And a second time they say, Hallelujah. And her smoke goeth up for ever and ever. 19:4 And the four and twenty elders and the four living creatures fell down and worshipped God that sitteth on the throne, saying, Amen; Hallelujah. 19:5And a voice came forth from the throne, saying, Give praise to our God, all ye

his servants, ye that fear him, the small and the great. 19:6 And I heard as it were the voice of a great multitude, and as the voice of many waters, and as the voice of mighty thunders, saying, Hallelujah: for the Lord our God, the Almighty, reigneth. 19:7 Let us rejoice and be exceeding glad, and let us give the glory unto him: for the marriage of the Lamb is come, and his wife hath made herself ready. 19:8 And it was given unto her that she should array herself in fine linen, bright and pure: for the fine linen is the righteous acts of the saints. 19:9 And he saith unto me, Write, (I'm writing, I'm writing," I said,) Blessed are they that are bidden to the marriage supper of the Lamb. And he saith unto me, These are true words of God. 19:10 And I fell down before his feet to worship him. And he saith unto me, See thou do it not: I am a fellow-servant with thee and with thy brethren that hold the testimony of the holy guy we used to call Jesus: worship his father; for the testimony of the former Jesus is the spirit of prophecy. 19:11 And I saw the heaven opened; and behold, a white horse, and he that sat thereon called Faithful and True; and in righteous he doth judge and make war. 19:12 And his eyes are a flame of fire, and upon his head are many diadems; and he hath a name written which no one knoweth but he himself. How do I know it was a name, then? Who's writing the story here? You or me? 19:13 And he is arrayed in a garment sprinkled with blood: and his name is called The Word of God. 19:14 And the armies which are in heaven followed him upon white horses, clothed in fine linen, white and pure. 19:15 And out of his mouth proceedeth a sharp sword, that with it he should smite the nations: and he shall rule them with a rod of iron: and he treadeth the winepress of the fierceness of the wrath of God, the Almighty. 19:16 And he hath on his garment and on his thigh a name written, KINGS OF KINGS, AND LORD OF LORDS. I thought the thigh was a strange place to have a name written, but I had seen so many things by this point, I stopped wondering. 19:17 And I saw an angel standing in the sun; and he cried with a loud voice, saying to all the birds that fly in mid heaven, Come and be gathered together unto the great supper of God; 19:18 that ye may eat the flesh of kings, and the flesh of captains, and the flesh of mighty men, and the flesh of horses and of them that sit thereon, and the flesh of all men, both free and bond, and small and great. "Yummy," the birds replied. 19:19 And I saw the beast, and the kings of the earth, and their armies, gathered together to make war against him that sat upon the horse, and against his army. 19:20 And the beast was taken, and with him the false prophet that wrought the signs in his sight, wherewith he deceived them that had received the mark of the beast and them that worshipped his image: they two were cast alive into the lake of fire that burneth with brimstone: 19:21 and the rest were killed with the sword of him that sat upon the horse, even the sword which came forth out of his mouth: and all the birds were filled with their flesh. Such fat, happy little flesh-eating birds.

Revelations 20

20:1 And I saw an angel coming down out of heaven, having the key of the abyss and a great chain in his hand. 20:2 And he laid hold on the dragon, the old serpent, which is the Devil and Satan, or EffDeeAr if you will, and bound him for a thousand years, 20:3 and cast him into the abyss, and shut it, and sealed it over him, that he should deceive the nations no more, until the thousand years should be finished: after this he must be loosed for a little time. Nobody really knows why. 20:4 And I saw thrones, and they sat upon them, and judgment was given unto them: and I saw the souls of them that had been beheaded for the testimony of he who, until recently was known by the moniker Jesus, and for the word of God, and such as worshipped not the beast, neither his image, and received not the mark upon their forehead and upon their hand; and they lived, and reigned with Christ a thousand years. 20:5 The rest of the dead lived not until the thousand years should be finished. This is the first resurrection. 20:6 Blessed and holy is he that hath part in the first resurrection: over these the second death hath no power; but they shall be priests of God and of Christ, and shall reign with him a thousand years. 20:7 And when the thousand years are finished, Satan shall be loosed out of his prison, 20:8 and shall come forth to deceive the nations which are in the four corners of the earth, Gog and Magog, to gather them together to the war: the number of whom is as the sand of the sea. 20:9 And they went up over the breadth of the earth, and compassed the camp of the saints about, and the beloved city: and fire came down out of heaven, and devoured them. You'd think they'd have learned the first time. 20:10 And the devil that deceived them was cast into the lake of fire and brimstone, where are also the beast and the false prophet; and they shall be tormented day and night for ever and ever. 20:11 And I saw a great white throne, and him that sat upon it, from whose face the earth and the heaven fled away; and there was found no place for them. 20:12 And I saw the dead, the great and the small, standing before the throne; and books were opened: and another book was opened, which is the book of life: and the dead were judged out of the things which were written in the books, according to their works. 20:13 And the sea gave up the dead that were in it; and death and Hades gave up the dead that were in them: and they were judged every man according to their works. 20:14 And death and Hades were cast into the lake of fire. This is the second death, even the lake of fire. 20:15 And if any was not found written in the book of life, he was cast into the lake of fire.

Revelations 21

21:1 And I saw a new heaven and a new earth: for the first heaven and the first earth are passed away; and the sea is no more. 21:2 And I saw the holy city, new Washyngtun, coming down out of heaven of God, made ready as a bride adorned for her husband. 21:3 And I heard a great voice out of the throne saying, Behold, the tabernacle of God is with men, and he shall dwell with them, and they shall be his peoples, and God himself shall be with them, and be their God: 21:4 and you shall know him by his name of old, that being Ronaldus Maximus, and he shall wipe away every tear from their eyes; and death shall be no more; neither shall there be mourning, nor crying, nor pain, nor burdensome taxes any more: the first things are passed away. 21:5 And he that sitteth on the throne said in a homey, self-effacing, chuckling voice, "Well, behold! I make all things new." And he saith, Write! (I'm writing, I'm writing, Mr. President," I said): for these words are faithful and true. 21:6 And he said unto me, They are come to pass. I am the Alpha and the Omega, the beginning and the end. I will give unto him that is athirst of the fountain of the water of life freely. 21:7 He that overcometh shall inherit these things; and I will be his God, and he shall be my son. 21:8 But for the fearful, and unbelieving, and abominable, and murderers, and fornicators, and sorcerers, and idolaters, and all liars, those who would cheat the wealthy of their money by unfair taxes, their part shall be in the lake that burneth with fire and brimstone; which is the second death. 21:9 And there came one of the seven angels who had the seven bowls, who were laden with the seven last plagues; and he spake with me, saying, Come hither, I will show thee the bride, the wife of the Lamb. 21:10 And he carried me away in the Spirit to a mountain great and high, and showed me the holy city Washyngtun, coming down out of heaven from God, 21:11 having the glory of God: her light was like unto a stone most precious, as it were a jasper stone, clear as crystal: 21:12 having a wall great and high; having twelve gates, and at the gates twelve angels; and names written thereon, which are the names of the twelve tribes of the children of what we would in the future call by the name "America": 21:13 on the east were three gates; and on the north three gates; and on the south three gates; and on the west three gates. So, yeah, that's twelve. 21:14 And the wall of the city had twelve foundations, and on them twelve names of the twelve apostles of the Lamb: They were Bush I, Chay-Nee, Bush II, Weinberger, Rumsfeld, Oliver of the North, Lim-Baugh, Roopert the Murdock, Condoleeza Converted Rice, Kahrl Rohve, and Beck of the Glenn. 21:15 And he that spake with me had for a measure a golden reed to measure the city, and the gates thereof, and the wall thereof. 21:16 And the city lieth foursquare, and the length thereof is as great as the breadth: and he measured the city with the reed, twelve thousand furlongs: the length and the breadth and the height thereof are equal. 21:17 And he measured the wall thereof, a hundred and forty and four cubits, according to the measure of a man, that is, of an angel. 21:18 And the building of the wall thereof was jasper: and the city was pure gold, like unto pure glass. 21:19 The foundations of the wall of the city were adorned with all manner of precious stones. The first foundation was jasper; the second, sapphire; the third, chalcedony; the fourth, emerald; 21:20 the fifth, sardonyx; the sixth, sardius; the seventh, chrysolite; the eighth, beryl; the ninth, topaz; the tenth, chrysoprase; the eleventh, jacinth; the twelfth, amethyst. 21:21 And the twelve gates were twelve pearls; each one of the several gates was of one pearl: and the street of the city was pure gold, as it were transparent glass. But who really cares? Do you? I sure didn't. But I was told to write. So I wrote. 21:22 And I saw no temple therein: for the Lord God the Almighty, and Ronaldus Maximus, are the temple thereof. 21:23 And the city hath no need of the sun, neither of the moon, to shine upon it: for the glory of God did lighten it, and the lamp thereof is the heavenly glow from the self-effacing smile of Ronaldus Maximus. 21:24 And the nations shall walk amidst the light thereof: and the kings of the earth bring their glory into it. 21:25 And the gates thereof shall in no wise be shut by day (for there shall be no night there): 21:26 and they shall bring the glory and the honor of the nations into it: 21:27 and there shall in no wise enter into it anything unclean, or he that maketh an abomination and a lie: but only they that are written in the book of life.

Revelations 22

22:1 And he showed me a river of water of life, bright as crystal, proceeding out of the throne of God and of the Ronaldus Maximus, 22:2 in the midst of the street thereof. And on this side of the river and on that was the tree of life, bearing twelve manner of fruits, yielding its fruit every month: and the leaves of the tree were for the healing of the nations. 22:3 And there shall be no curse any more: and the throne of God and of the Ronaldus Maximus shall be therein: and his servants shall serve him; 22:4 and they shall see his face; and his name shall be on their foreheads. 22:5 And there shall be night no more; and they need no light of lamp, neither light of sun; for the Lord God shall give them light: and they shall reign for ever and ever. 22:6 And he said unto me, These words are faithful and true: and the Lord, the God of the spirits of the prophets, sent his angels to show unto his servants the things which must shortly come to pass. 22:7 And behold, I come quickly. Blessed is he that keepeth the words of the prophecy of this book. 22:8 And I John am he that heard and saw these things. And when I heard and saw, I fell down to worship before the feet of the angel that showed me these things. 22:9 And he saith unto me, See thou do it not: I am a fellow-servant with thee and with thy brethren the prophets, and with them that keep the words of this book: worship God. 22:10 And he saith unto me, Seal not up the words of the prophecy of this book; for the time is at hand. 22:11 He that is unrighteous, let him do unrighteousness still: and he that is filthy, let him be made filthy still: and he that is righteous, let him do righteousness still: and he that is holy,

let him be made holy still. 22:12 Behold, I come quickly; and my reward is with me, to render to each man according as his work is.

22:13 I am Ronaldus Maximus, the first and the last, the beginning and the end. 22:14Blessed are they that wash their robes, that they may have the right to come to the tree of life, and may enter in by the gates into the city. 22:15Without are the dogs, and the sorcerers, and the fornicators, and the murderers, and the idolaters, and the liberals, and every one that loveth and maketh a lie. 22:16 I, Ronaldus Maximus, have sent mine angel to testify unto you these things for the churches. I am the root and the offspring of the Gold Water, the bright, the morning star. 22:17 And the Spirit and the bride say, Come. And he that heareth, let him say, Come. And he that is at thirst, let him come: he that will, let him take the water of life freely. 22:18 I testify unto every man that heareth the words of the prophecy of this book, if any man shall add unto them, God shall add unto him the plagues which are written in this book: 22:19 and if any man shall take away from the words of the book of this prophecy, God shall take away his part from the tree of life, and out of the holy city, which are written in this book. 22:20 He who testifieth these things saith, Yea: I come quickly. Amen: come, Lord Ronaldus. 22:21 The grace of the Lord Ronaldus be with the saints. Amen. And he was gone. And all that remained was a ream of scribbled-upon paper and a massive headache. No more mushrooms. I mean it this time

13 THE PUNCH LINE

Of course you realize there is no "newly-revealed Word of God." I was as sincere about that as Stephen Colbert is sincere about being a conservative. Heck, even the commonly accepted "word of God" is anything BUT "the word of God." It's a "Bible by Committee".

As I wrote earlier, the King James Version was created by a group of scholars in the early 1600's to give the "common people" a bible they could understand, one that could be read at church. One they could hold on to as their own.

Even the original texts used to cobble a Bible together were not written by "God." They were written by men. And we're not even sure WHICH men, but they were written by men with an agenda and nowhere does it say that God held the pen. The four commonly-accepted Gospels, for instance. They're not written by who you think wrote them.

Scholars tend to agree that the Gospel of Mark was not written by an eyewitness to the actual events. The Gospel of Matthew was likely written by some guy named Papias some 100 years after Jesus died, based on a collection of quotations of Jesus collected by Matthew. The Gospel of Luke is believed by many to have been written by another person who never

laid eyes on Jesus or heard a word he said. I mean, look at the preface!

1 Forasmuch as many have taken in hand to set forth in order a declaration of those things which are most surely believed among us, 2 Even as they delivered them unto us, which from the beginning were eyewitnesses, and ministers of the word; 3 It seemed good to me also, having had perfect understanding of all things from the very first, to write unto thee in order,

most excellent Theophilus 4 That thou mightest know the certainty of those things, wherein thou hast been instructed.
LUKE 1:1-4 (KJV)

Now LATER versions of the Bible translate THIS into saying that the writer was THERE and HE is transmitting this information based on his own account. And therein lies the problem with the sacred, unerring, eternal word of God. It's been rewritten so many times, and the meanings of the words undergo subtle changes with each revision. Consider this chart:

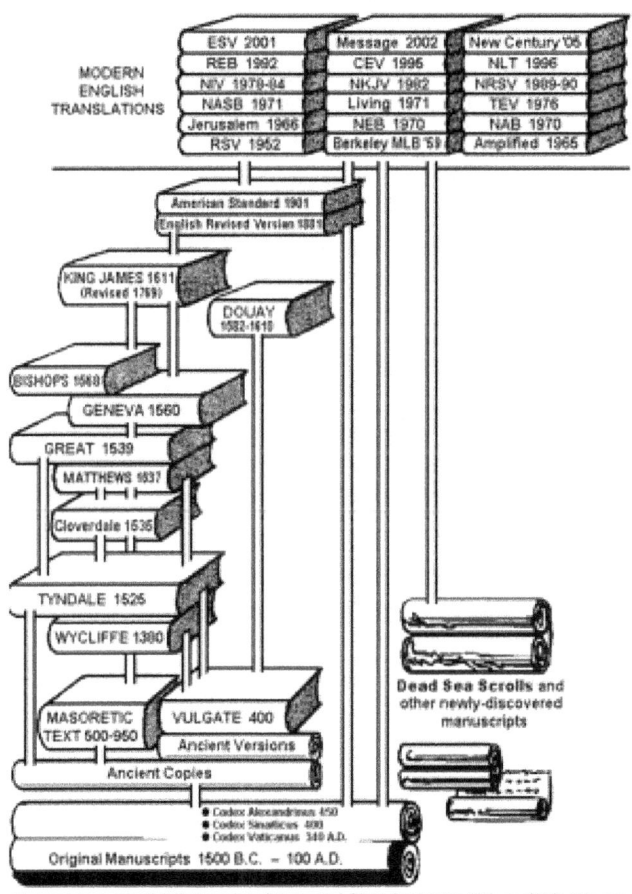

You know the old parlor game where one person starts a story by telling it to the person next to him. By the time the story goes all the way around the circle, it is unrecognizable when compared to the original version.

But be that as it may. The Bible is a nice book of stories that tells of an angry and vengeful God who wrought his wrath on the wicked and slew the enemies of the just and dashed their enemies babies against trees and all manner of good, bloody whatnot. In the New Testament, God has had a lobotomy or a laxative, because now he's the good and kind and gentle Father who sent his only begotten son (a premise for which Joseph, Mary's husband, should win "Father of the Year" award for swallowing the "God Made Me Pregnant" story) to live his life in abject poverty then die a brutal, painful death so that we can go to heaven just by believing this happened and accepting that he did it for our sins.

Yet, we keep sinning and sinning and sinning like never before, and the people who purport to believe in the word-for-word truthfulness of the Bible sin right alongside of us.

There's one sin that Tea Partiers don't have any problem with whatsoever. "Bearing False Witness." In her July 2010 article for the Project Syndicate website, libertarian social critic Naomi Wolf calls out God for "Crashing the Tea Party."[13] And she starts out with a few doozies of her own.

For instance…

The Tea Party emerged from a laudably grassroots base: libertarians, fervent Constitutionalists, and ordinary people alarmed at the suppression of liberties, whether by George W. Bush or Barack Obama. Libertarians, of course, tend to understand church-state separation: if you

---

[13] http://www.project-syndicate.org/commentary/wolf26/English

don't want government intruding in your life, you definitely don't want it telling you how to worship.

Now, Naomi, that's just not true. If you want to write a column about a movement being co-opted by religious zealots, ought you not cleave to the truth in what you write? The Tea Party movement was started and financed[14] by several non-profit and for profit organizations:

501©(4) Non-Profit Organizations: Tea Party Patriots, an organization with more than 1,000 affiliated groups across the nation that proclaims itself to be the "Official Home of the Tea Party Movement; Americans For Prosperity, a grassroots organization founded by David H. Koch in 2003, and led by Tim Phillips. The group has over 1 million members in 500 local affiliates, and led protests against health care reform in 2009. FreedomWorks, an organization led Dick Armey. Like Americans For Prosperity, the group has over 1 million members in 500 local affiliates. It makes local and national candidate endorsements. Tea Party Express, a national bus tour run by Our Country Deserves Better PAC, itself a conservative political action committee created by Sacramento-based Republican consulting firm Russo, Marsh, and Associates; For-Profit Businesses: Tea Party Nation, which sponsored the National Tea Party Convention that was criticized for its $549 ticket price and because Sarah Palin was apparently paid $100,000 for her appearance (which she put towards SarahPAC).

So please, Naomi, spare us the "grassroots" nonsense. But a lot of the other stuff you wrote in your column? Dead on!

Unfortunately, religious bigotry also has a long history in America, and there are powerful factions that cannot accept that God did not intend the US to be a Christian

---

[14] http://en.wikipedia.org/wiki/Tea_Party_movement

nation. Ronald Reagan saw the benefit of tapping these constituencies, introducing a faith-first element into what had been a more secularized, "big tent" conservatism.

Since the 1980's, "culture wars" (usually staged) about homosexuality, abortion, and sex education, or other coded messaging about religious values, have served to mobilize the religious right. Bush's early avowal of his conversion experience was given in language poll-tested for acceptance by fundamentalist Christians.

Right on, sister. A quick Google check will come up with dozens of examples of Thomas Jefferson saying things that Thomas Jefferson never said. You'll find all sorts of examples of founding fathers saying that America was intended to be a Christian nation, only to take a closer look and see what they said was taken out of context or was never uttered in the first place.

Also from Ms. Wolf's column...

At Townhall.com and LibertyCentral.org, for example, explanations of the Constitution sit uneasily next to articles urging citizens to take action against the construction of a mosque at the Twin Towers site in New York. Elsewhere, a seemingly commendable grassroots petition movement to re-establish Constitutional values at the state level turns out to be – if you read the fine print – a drive to enshrine Christian values in state law.

Likewise, the Tea Party, which showed no interest in racist language or iconography at its outset, increasingly injects such demagoguery into its messages. The movement's libertarian message is now regularly subverted by anti-Muslim paranoia and contradicted by activism supporting such initiatives as the mass round-up,

"And the day will come when the mystical generation of Jesus, by the supreme being as his father in the womb of a virgin, will be classed with the fable of the generation of Minerva in the brain of Jupiter" (In a letter to John Adams, April 11, 1823).

without due process, of undocumented immigrants in Arizona.

Amen and amen. Verily I say unto you that the right wing is using the Bible as a cudgel to beat in the brains of those who would stand in the way of this conservative, industrialist-funded, Tea Party effort to take away the rights of people who don't see the world through the same "stained with the blood of the Lamb" glasses as they.

Unfortunately, when faced with choosing between a comfortable falsehood and an irritating truth.

Conservatives tend to prefer to cling to the comfortable falsehood. This is nothing new. Ever since the founding of the nation, certain elements have been insisting that America, by her very nature and at the behest of her founding fathers, was INTENDED to be a Christian Nation. For example...

More than half of self-identified Tea Party members say America is a Christian nation, while just over four out of 10 white evangelicals believe that - the same as the proportion of the general population that says so.

Nearly half of Tea Partiers believe the Bible is the literal word of God, for example. One in three Americans overall believes that, while nearly two in three white evangelicals do.

Tea Partiers are much more likely than white evangelicals or Americans in general to think that minorities get too much attention from the government.

Almost six in 10 Tea Partiers believe that, while fewer than four in 10 white evangelicals say so. Figures for white evangelicals and Americans in general on that question are statistically identical.

But Tea Party opinions of immigrants line up with those of white evangelicals, with just under two out of three in each group saying immigrants are a burden on the U.S. "because they take jobs, housing and health care."

Just under half of the population as a whole says that.[15]

---

[15] http://religion.blogs.cnn.com/2010/10/05/most-tea-partiers-call-america-a-christian-nation-study-finds/

This concept is demonstrably false. America was founded as a nation where ALL religions were to be tolerated as well as the right to be non-religious.

There is much written on the subject to support this theory.

The primary leaders of the so-called founding fathers of our nation were not Bible-believing Christians; they were deists. Deism was a philosophical belief that was widely accepted by the colonial intelligentsia at the time of the American Revolution. Its major tenets included belief in human reason as a reliable means of solving social and political problems and belief in a supreme deity who created the universe to operate solely by natural laws. The supreme God of the Deists removed himself entirely from the universe after creating it. They believed that he assumed no control over it, exerted no influence on natural phenomena, and gave no supernatural revelation to man. A necessary consequence of these beliefs was a rejection of many doctrines central to the Christian religion. Deists did not believe in the virgin birth, divinity, or resurrection of Jesus, the efficacy of prayer, the miracles of the Bible, or even the divine inspiration of the Bible.[16]

...the Treaty of Tripoli, ratified by the U.S. Senate in 1797. Article 11 states: "As the Government of the United States of America is not, in any sense, founded on the Christian religion; as it has in itself no character of enmity against the laws, religion, or tranquility [sic], of Mussulmen [Muslims]; and, as the said States never have entered into any war, or act of hostility against any

---

16

http://www.infidels.org/library/modern/farrell_till/myth.html

Mahometan nation, it is declared by the parties, that no pretext arising from religious opinions, shall ever produce an interruption of the harmony existing between the two countries."

Conservatives who claim that the U.S. is a "Christian nation" sometimes dismiss the Treaty of Tripoli because it was authored by the U.S. diplomat Joel Barlow, an Enlightenment freethinker. Well, then, how about the tenth president, John Tyler, in an 1843 letter: "The United States have adventured upon a great and noble experiment, which is believed to have been hazarded in the absence of all previous precedent -- that of total separation of Church and State. No religious establishment by law exists among us. The conscience is left free from all restraint and each is permitted to worship his Maker after his own judgment. The offices of the Government are open alike to all. No tithes are levied to support an established Hierarchy, nor is the fallible judgment of man set up as the sure and infallible creed of faith. The Mohammedan, if he will to come among us would have the privilege guaranteed to him by the constitution to worship according to the Koran; and the East Indian might erect a shrine to Brahma, if it so pleased him. Such is the spirit of toleration inculcated by our political Institutions."

...

Here's George Washington in a letter to the Hebrew Congregation of Newport, Rhode Island in 1790: "The citizens of the United States of America have a right to applaud themselves for having given to mankind examples of an enlarged and liberal policy -- a policy worthy of imitation. All possess alike liberty of conscience and immunities of citizenship. It is now no more that toleration is spoken of as if it were the indulgence of one class of people that another enjoyed the exercise of their inherent natural rights, for, happily, the Government of the United States, which gives to bigotry no sanction, to

persecution no assistance, requires only that they who live under its protection should demean themselves as good citizens in giving it on all occasions their effectual support ... May the children of the stock of Abraham who dwell in this land continue to merit and enjoy the good will of the other inhabitants -- while every one shall sit in safety under his own vine and fig tree and there shall be none to make him afraid."[17]

Andrew Jackson resisted bids in the 1820s to form a "Christian party in politics." Abraham Lincoln buried a proposed "Christian amendment" to the Constitution to declare the nation's fealty to Jesus. Theodore Roosevelt defended William Howard Taft, a Unitarian, from religious attacks by supporters of William Jennings Bryan.

The founders were not anti-religion. Many of them were faithful in their personal lives, and in their public language they evoked God. They grounded the founding principle of the nation — that all men are created equal — in the divine. But they wanted faith to be one thread in the country's tapestry, not the whole tapestry.[18]

It's appallingly hypocritical for Mr. Gingrich to claim that secular Americans "do not understand America" while he intentionally distorts and misrepresents our government's founding document simply to score cheap political points with a religious constituency. In recent speeches, Gingrich has assaulted the secular character of our government while at the same time condemning the possibility of a theocratic regime in Egypt headed by the Muslim Brotherhood. Why does he think secular government is good for Egyptians but not Americans?

Of course, Mr. Gingrich is not the only likely GOP presidential contender who has made veiled calls for an

---

17

http://www.salon.com/news/opinion/feature/2009/04/14/christian_nation

18

http://www.nytimes.com/2007/10/07/opinion/07meacham.html

American theocracy based on his particular brand of Christianity.

At the same Iowa event that Gingrich spoke at Monday, former Minnesota Gov. Tim Pawlenty said, "We need to be a country that turns toward God. Not a country that turns away from God." Well, whose god is he referring to? Sixteen percent of Americans ascribe to no religion, and there are millions of Muslim, Hindu, Sikh and Buddhist Americans whose religious views do not include the same Judeo-Christian "God" that Pawlenty suggests should be forced on all citizens. Our population may be majority Christian, but as stated in the Treaty of Tripoli, signed by President John Adams in 1797, "the Government of the United States of America is not, in any sense, founded on the Christian religion."

Rather, the United States was founded on secular values, such as equality, democracy and religious liberty, designed to prevent Americans from imposing their personal religious views on one another — or on our government.

Misguided and historically inaccurate calls for a more theocratic America represent a threat to the very freedoms the Constitution granted to all Americans — Gingrich and Pawlenty included.[19]

I could go on and on and fill pages with similar material gleaned from all manner of sources. But what good would it do? But like I said, when given the choice between a comfortable lie and an irritating truth, Conservatives cling to the comfortable lie. No matter HOW much proof you place before them, they insist on the lie. It's a lie they LIKE! It's a

---

[19] http://thehill.com/opinion/letters/148843-constitution-is-clear-us-is-not-a-christian-nation

lie that supports their political point of view. It's comfortable. They clutch it like a child clutches a teddy bear.

Now, the NEAT thing about all of this is that YOU, as an AMERICAN are free to make your OWN choices on such matters as religion. This is not Iran. Neither is it Israel. A country founded on freedom OF religion must also, logically, be founded on freedom FROM religion!

I'm not an atheist, nor am I a traditional religionist. I do believe there is a central force for good in the universe, but I don't think this force has (or NEEDS) a name — other than what we choose to call it.

As humans, our understanding is limited to the things we are capable of understanding. Many a marijuana-scented rambling discussion around a teenaged campfire discussing the concept of eternity has convinced me that we are incapable of grasping the meaning of the word "eternal." Our lives have beginnings and endings. Just like our days, our weekends, our favorite TV shows. We can not wrap our heads around something that never began and never will end. And that includes "God." A human being can have no more conception of "God" or "God's will" than my dogs do about why I can't make it stop raining when they want to go outside. Our knowledge and ability to learn is only limited by our mortality. Saying that something is "God's will" is intellectual laziness.

It is not "God's will" that three of my siblings died in their 40s and 50s, as did my father. It was not "God's will" that one of my grandfathers — not a good man by any measure of the word — lived into his mid 90s. It is not "God's will" that I have Parkinson's disease.

These things happen because they happen. In some cases, they happen because we eat and drink and smoke things we shouldn't eat or drink or smoke. But sometimes, even with a perfect diet, a healthy liver and the pink and clean lungs of a 2-year old, we get cancer. We blow a blood vessel. Something goes wrong in the dopamine producing portion of our brains, and we get Parkinson's. This is not the will of a God who watches over us all and determines our every move, who knows what we're gonna do before we do it — thereby putting the lie to the whole concept of "free will." That "God" cannot exist outside the doctrines of those who use this angry, omnipotent being as a "Big Daddy Who Will Spank!"

As I said, I believe there is a central force of good that holds things together. But that force does not get involved in our day to day activities.

To quote a popular bumper sticker — "Shit Happens."

I believe the popular Judeo-Christian and Islamic concept of "God" has been adulterated to be used as a cudgel to punish "bad" behavior and to scare folks into toeing the line. Consider the concept of "Hell." Then think about how much you love your children, your family, your mother and father, your siblings. Then compare that love you feel to the "perfect love" we have been drilled into believing God has for each and every one of us. Could YOU condemn someone you love with your human, imperfect love to an eternity of torment? I am far from a perfect being, but I can't discipline my dogs for more than 5 minutes without feeling bad about it.

I'm not saying that this "central force" I believe in doesn't love us. I'm saying that it's far too busy to take all that much notice.

I do pray. And when I pray, it's NOT to ask for a direct result or a "thing" I want. I pray that I am able to tap into this "goodness" in the universe for the strength to deal with the obstacles that are in my way. I put energy back into this "goodness" by being thankful for the good things, for my blessings, for a beautiful sunset, a rainbow, for the safe conclusion of a trip.

I believe there is a fundamental "goodness" in the Universe and that we all have the potential to evolve to become a part of it. We have to want to evolve. We have to want to move past the anger and hatred and prejudice and fear we've been indoctrinated into accepting as normal parts of our existence. We have to understand that bad things happen to good people, good things happen to bad people, and that's just how it is. When Pat Robertson "prayed away" that hurricane that was heading toward his cable TV studio, did that mean the people who were killed further up the coast were less "worthy" or "righteous"? When Robertson and Falwell said that 9/11 and Katrina happened because God was mad at all the gayness and abortion in America, why did he "take" so many heterosexuals, pregnant women and folks who would no sooner have an abortion than willingly have an eyeball removed? What kind of psychotic God is this they preach?

That God is a creation of man. Therefore, it is an imperfect and flawed creation.

Please understand, this is MY concept. It does not have to be yours! In fact, it SHOULDN'T be yours. You are a free, sentient being, capable (if you choose) of coming up with your own answers and reasons for the things that are beyond our ken as mortal humans.

I believe there have been enlightened teachers in our past, such as Buddha, Jesus, Confucius, Gandhi (Mahatma, not Indira) and others we don't know about and will never hear about because no one wrote about them.

I believe there are more good people than bad, but I also believe there are more stupid people than smart. And I believe it is the stupid people who are keeping the rest of us down. And that stupidity is grounded in fear.

There are people who fear homosexuality, therefore they ban gay marriage. There are people who fear that which is different from them, that which does not look like them or talk like them or observe the same holidays they do. That explains racism, cultural prejudice, and the majority of evil on the planet. That explains the conflict between Christian and Jew, between Christian and Muslim, between Muslim and Jew and the never-ending urge to kill each other because THEY don't have the same "inside track" towards "God" that we do.

Stupid people wrap themselves in symbols, declare those symbols as "good" and "better than other symbols." In our case, as Americans, it's the concept of "American Exceptionalism" — that just because we are Americans, we are "Chosen of God" and therefore better than everyone else, and everyone had better get out of our way and do what we tell them or there's gonna be trouble.

Evil people who wish to enrich themselves at the expense of the stupid do so by telling us how CORRECT our stupidity is! It's RIGHT that we fear, that we hate, that we are suspicious, because look what happens when you let BAD people into the country. 9/11 is their talisman. We are told it's RIGHT that we give up rights because those rights are KEEPING THEM from KEEPING US SAFE! Never mind that around 3,000 people died on 9/11, while over 4,000 have been killed in a war we were told was waged BECAUSE of 9/11 that had nothing to DO with 9/11 while the real perpetrators of the attack were allowed to escape into the mountains of our great ally, Pakistan.

3,000 were killed on 9/11 and the stupid people enabled the evil people who convinced us that our stupidity would keep us safe. Don't ask questions. Never mind that the American Cancer Society says 6 million will die in 2010 because of smoking. 3,000 were killed on 9/11. Never mind that there were 16,000 drunk driving deaths in 2006. 3,000 died on 9/11!

It's "God's Will."

Have you ever considered that the more educated a person is, the more books he or she reads, the more he or she has traveled in the world, the less likely that person is to be afraid? Of other people? Of other ideas? The more narrowly one confines oneself in the arena of culture and awareness, the more likely that person is to be afraid of "enemies" that "lurk" and are "waiting to take advantage" of our "weakness"?

An old, and now deceased, friend of mine said it best. "What a better world this would be if stupid people realized it is better to be smart."

And if I may adapt a phrase to my own purposes, there is none more stupid than he or she who will not learn.

Now, these same forces of stupidity are working overtime to ensure that health insurance companies continue to rake in windfall profits at the expense of stupid people who think that "gubbermint health care" is "socialist."

Millionaires like Rush Limbaugh and Sean Hannity and Glenn Beck convince their viewers and listeners to embrace their fear, to hold onto it tight for it will keep them safe. (And poor, and sick, and uneducated and stupid, they neglect to add…)

If we have a purpose in this life, it's to love and be loved. And who we love and how we love is nobody's business but our own. It is our mandate to learn as much as we can and to pass that knowledge on to the next generation so they may add to it and pass their combined knowledge on to another, hopefully more enlightened, generation.

Our job is to get through this life in as happy a fashion as is possible, to help others achieve this happiness where possible, to smooth the way for our fellow travelers so that we may also enjoy as smooth a ride as possible.

Life is too short to be angry, to be afraid, to hate.

Life is FAR too short to embrace stupidity.

As Americans, we need to wake up to what's going on while there is still time. Unfortunately, the industrialist owners of the various mainstream media outlets, Viacom (CBS), GE/Comcast (NBC), Time Warner (CNN), Disney (ABC) and Rupert Murdoch's GOP Front organization at Fox News, are determined to keep you nice and sleepy and stupid as sheep. They understand that if you don't know what's really going on, you won't get angry about it. They understand that if they give you cute little stories about doggies and kitties and royal weddings and balloon boys and whatever else captures the attention of the average American who thinks "Entertainment Tonight" is the REAL news, then they can dismantle, piece by piece, the fabric of freedom in this country.

This book, my column on Technorati[20], my blog[21], these are all just a tiny shifting of the bed covers in what I hope will become a nationwide awakening. I know rousing from a long nap is unpleasant. You're groggy, you're still foggy-headed and there's nothing you'd like better than to just slip back under the covers and go back to sleep.

---

[20] http://technorati.com/politics/feature/troll/

[21] http://parkypundit.com

But you really, really DO need to wake up and protect yourselves, and your country, from these thieves who will rob you in broad daylight.

For as it is written:

Your rulers are rebels, partners with thieves; they all love bribes and chase after gifts. They do not defend the cause of the fatherless; the widow's case does not come before them.

ISAIAH 1:23

So then, what of the basic question put to the reader by the title of this book? Can you BE a Tea Party Member and STILL Call Yourself a "Christian"? Can you subscribe to a political philosophy that calls for the disenfranchisement of the poor and middle class while continuing to give tax breaks to the wealthy? Can you belong to an organization that would deny universal health care to all Americans? Can you BE a Christian and be part of an organization that fundamentally flies into the face of practically everything Jesus taught during his Earthly ministry?

The answer? Yes. Of course you can. This is America. You can call yourself whatever you want.

Of course, you'll be a hypocrite..

ABOUT THE AUTHOR

It's been an interesting career.

I've been a radio disc jockey, news director, program director, talk show host, and I was one of the original broadcasters at XM Satellite Radio. I've been a newspaper editor, writer, reporter and columnist. In between radio and news gigs, I drove 18-wheeler for a living.

I eventually found myself working for the federal government, as a writer-editor with the Clinical Center at the National Institutes of Health, a job from which I was forced by Parkinson's disease in March 2011.

Parkinson's disease...

It was just about three weeks after my 45th birthday in 2000 when I was diagnosed with Parkinson's disease. In 2007 while working at a federal agency as a writer and podcaster, telling other people about the importance of clinical trials, I heard about and volunteered for an experimental brain surgery to determine whether or not "deep brain stimulation" could be done on patients in the earlier stages of the disease.

The purpose of the clinical trial is to prove that DBS, when done earlier in the progression of the disease, might just slow down or stop the degeneration that is an inevitable part of the disease.

I currently blog about my PD experiences and I write satire about world and national politics. I have a left-wing point of view and little patience for tea party nonsense. Feel free to check my blog, share your comments and just "hello"!

Bill Schmalfeldt

OTHER BOOKS BY BIL SCHMALFELDT

PUT ON YOUR PARKY FACE

"Telling his own story of facing the disease and what he's done to try to make the most of it, "Put on Your Parky Face" is a thoughtful take on the side of Parkinson's disease rarely heard."

Bill Schmalfeldt is serving notice. It's time for Parkinson's disease patients to stop being invisible. It's time for a nationwide effort to raise awareness about crippling degenerative neurological disorder and the havoc it wreaks on American families — approximately 1.5 million people currently have a PD diagnosis with 50-thousand new cases each year. Having had PD himself since 2000 at age 45, Bill volunteered for experimental brain surgery in 2007. He spins a humorous, poignant, sometimes angry tale about his life with this incurable progressive neurological condition. He has retired from his job in the Federal service and plans to use his remaining time, focus and energy to help fund the research that will find the cure. In fact, 100% of the author proceeds from this book will be donated to Parkinson's research charities. This book should be owned by anyone who has Parkinson's, anyone who knows someone with PD, or anyone who might GET Parkinson's someday — in other words… YOU!

OUTRAGEOUS ACCUSATIONS AND DAMNABLE LIES

One of the lesser-discussed symptoms of Parkinson's disease is irritability. I was diagnosed with this degenerative neurological disorder three weeks after my 45th birthday in 2000. I have 11 years of irritability built up inside me. That's why I enjoy writing satire.

That's why I wrote "Outrageous Accusations and Damnable Lies".

After 11 years of this crap, my walking is affected. I lose my balance and fall easily. My ability to speak is hampered. Most folks with Parkinson's tend to develop a quiet, whispery, reedy voice. Not me! A loudmouth I was born and a loudmouth I shall die. No, my affliction is in the area of clarity. When I speak, all the words try to rush out in an unintelligible jumble. If I slow down and think of each word as I say it, things go a little easier. But as someone with 30+ years of radio broadcasting experience in my pocket, someone who has spent the last six years as a podcaster for the Federal Government, this loss of the ability to clearly express myself verbally without sounding like Porky Pig is frustrating to say the least.

That is why I enjoy writing. At this point in my progressive decline, it's still something I can do fairly well. And I particularly enjoy writing satire. Particularly political satire. Particularly satire that perforates the smug attitude of the American Conservative mindset. I find fault with almost everyone! (Makes me a fun guy to hang out with!) The religiofascist and the assured atheist are just as likely to suffer under my keyboard. Anyone who thinks he or she knows ANYTHING for an absolute certainty and beyond questioning is a target. If you read an essay here that annoys or inflames you… good.

Read the next essay. You might like that one. Or, at any rate, you'll have something to think about.

If you're the kind of person who has absolute certainty in your religion, your patriotism, American Exceptionalism, tread lightly between these book covers. Take a deep breath. They're just words.

And aren't words MAGICAL things?

The offerings herein are divided into four broad categories...

Dumbasses

Knuckleheads

Media

Odds and Ends.

A full listing of essays can be found in the Table of Contents.

Thanks to the editors at Technorati.com for providing first publication for the vast majority of these works. I take full responsibility for my own words, whether I meant them sincerely or not.

And that's part of the fun about reading satire... how much of what you're reading is based on YOUR preconceived notions, and how much is based on the writer's? Let's see, shall we?

Also available at Amazon as a paperback and Kindle book.

Imagine the biblical book of Revelations, rewritten by Woody Allen or Mel Brooks.

End Times: A Comedy in Two Acts, has more laughs in each scene than the ENTIRE Left Behind series. Co-playwrights and twin brothers Bill and Bob Schmalfeldt worked on this project. Bill has other books on Lulu — notably, Put On Your Parky Face, Hunky Dunk, and Undercover Trucker: How I Saved America by Truckin' Towels for the Taliban.

Sadly, Bob passed away in 2004.

Proceeds from this work will be shared with his widow, Lori.

HUNKY DUNK

Mud and Jake Klemper were special boys.

Their father knew how special they were although his constant browbeating did little to encourage their special gift. But he did instill them with one thing: The Klemper Pride.

The boys would have lived their lives unknown and uncared about in Slope Oak, Iowa, if not for a little song Mud and Jake composed one hot afternoon. It became a monster hit. As a result of their success, the boys became international superstars.

Through it all, they never really seemed to understand what was going on around them and they maintained their simple outlook on life — until it all became too much!

A REVIEW:

Schmalfeldt's books always make you laugh while giving you something to think about. Mud and Jake Klemper are described as "special boys" on the cover. For the first half of "Hunky Dunk", you could be excused for thinking this is a funny, rollicking story about two "special"–as in "special needs"–brothers who unwittingly write a hit song and become famous. Think Chauncey Gardiner in Jerzy Kosinski's "Being There." Then the book becomes something else altogether and "special boys" takes on a whole new meaning. I don't want to give any spoilers, but it's a completely brilliant twist you never see coming that raises the book to a whole new level. It's insane, and very fun to read.

Undercover Trucker: How I Saved America by Truckin' Towels for the Taliban

Billy Big Rig has lived his life on The Killer Road. His many adventures (and marriages) have left him bruised, scarred, but unbroken.

In 2000 as a disgraced alcoholic 18-wheel driver, Billy redeemed himself by saving America.

He did this by infiltrating an Al Qaeda cell in prison and traveling with them to Afghanistan in the days leading up to 9/11. Then, if he is to be believed, he nearly single-handedly won the war, killed Saddam Hussein, took care of Osama bin Laden and had a fist fight with Bill Clinton.

For obvious reasons his real identity can never be revealed. His life remains in constant danger. But he tells his story for the first time in this hilarious first-hand account.

Along the way, you'll learn about his unique upbringing, his politically-incorrect philosophy, and how to survive when EVERYONE wants to kill you!.

A LITTLE LOVE FOR A BOOK I WROTE A LONG TIME AGO

You never forget your first! And "...by the people..." was my first published novel. It was published by Dead End Street, LLC in 2004, and I actually started writing it in 1998. Fiction by a new author was hard THEN to get published, and it's even harder NOW! The good folks at DES invested $500 in the sale of this little book, and they have yet to make their money back on the investment. If you're in the mood for a good, funny, slightly-outdated political potboiler to read this summer, I recommend "...by the people..."

So did these folks.

"The story of first-term congressman Roberto Huerta's quick rise through the US political system makes for a compelling fantasy. "...By The People..." manages to be funny and suspenseful while presenting some serious thoughts about integrity and true leadership. This book has a huge cast of characters, frequently switching viewpoints and speeding through an outrageous plot. While it skewers business as usual in DC, it mostly shies away from partisan politics and keeps from getting overly preachy. Some of the characters are a bit hastily drawn to serve the fast-moving plot, but Huerta and his underdog allies quickly grab your attention and have you rooting for them. A couple of tawdry sex scenes probably rule the book out for younger readers who might otherwise benefit from this book's view of Washington's inner workings."
–Harrison Wein

This wisecracking lightning-strike of a book romps through all the dangers of Washington, D.C., including its federal city and the neighborhoods we know. Like a medieval knight errant, Schmalfeldt's hero is incorruptible, indefatigable, irrepressible and... a real hard head. When this reluctant crusader rushes in to save the maiden, he leaves his flanks exposed and then ... Will the former wrestling-scholarship-boy pin the dragon to the mat?

If you like a fast, funny read that's not allergic to ideas; if you like politics that aren't allergic to hope; if you like K.C. Constantine, George V. Higgins and Elmore Leonard, try William M. Schmalfeldt. The guy writes like the bastard child of Molly Ivins and Charles Dickens. Can't wait for the sequel...
–Isabel Lewis

SYNOPSIS

With the Vice President's recent death and President DeWitt's health worsening by the day, the precarious balance of power between the Democratic President and a Republican-controlled Congress has moved to the right. Albert Wantner, the politically shrewd Speaker of the House, will ascend to the Presidency if the ill and elderly President dies before a new "veep" is appointed. For this reason, Wantner plans to delay Congressional approval of any candidate, and the President realizes that he must choose a person so politically pure that the public will clamor for his confirmation and punish Wantner for any delay.

Enter Roberto Huerta, a disillusioned first-term, Democratic congressman from Texas, who recently became American's newest celebrity by rescuing a woman from an assault by Washington street thugs. After some soul searching, Huerta accepts the President's offer, and a bitter – but ultimately successful – bid for Congressional approval takes place. Soon after Huerta is sworn in, the President drops a bombshell in a speech to a joint session of Congress, leaving a frightened and somewhat astonished Huerta struggling to establish a Capra-esque executive branch that is truly directed ***"…by the people…."***

ALL BOOKS SHOWN HERE ARE AVAILABLE AT MY PERSONAL BLOG, http://parkypundit.com, and can be purchased online either at Lulu.com, Amazon, Barnes & Noble, Books-a-Million or CreateSpace.com

www.ingramcontent.com/pod-product-compliance
Lightning Source LLC
Chambersburg PA
CBHW070643160426
43194CB00009B/1563